REVERSE THE CHARGES

REVERSE THE CHARGES

HOW TO SAVE MONEY ON YOUR PHONE BILL

Money-saving tips on: buying your own phone • comparing MCI, Sprint, MetroFone, ITT, and other long-distance services • wiring your own home • detecting hidden charges on your phone bill • and much more!

SAMUEL A. SIMON & JOSEPH W. WAZ, JR.
of the Telecommunications Research and Action Center

Introduction by Ralph Nader

Pantheon Books, New York

Library of Congress Cataloging in Publication Data

Simon, Sam, 1945—
Reverse the charges.

Rev. ed of: Reverse the charges / Joe Waz.
c1981.
Bibliography: p.
Includes index.
1. Telephone—United States—Consumer complaints.
2. American Telephone and Telegraph Company.
3. Consumer complaints—United States. I. Waz, Joe. II. Waz, Joe.
Reverse the charges. III. Title.

HE8817.S55   1983   384.6′3   82-48950
ISBN 0-394-71490-3 (pbk.)

Manufactured in the United States of America

Revised Edition, 1983

ACKNOWLEDGMENTS

This edition of *Reverse the Charges* would not have been possible without the assistance of the staff and interns of the Telecommunications Research and Action Center. Staff assistance has been provided by Laurie Drucker, Paul Stern, Bruce Jacobs, Pam Marks, and Leslie Bland. Intern assistance was provided by Mary Woods, Linda Naklicki, Nathan Goldberg, Toni Carpio, John Ketterer, and Ross Carr.

CONTENTS

REVERSE THE CHARGES

INTRODUCTION

Over 90 percent of the households in the U.S. have telephone service available to them. Telephone service today is recognized as one of the necessities of life.

Most people still rent their telephones from the telephone company (although they are no longer required to) and pay monthly rental charges, in addition to some form of usage charge, installation charge, and a basic service charge. The typical telephone bill does not break these charges down in much detail, so few people realize, for example, how they would benefit significantly if they simply bought and owned their own telephone.

Most people still purchase their long-distance telephone service from AT&T when, if they average $25 or more a month in long-distance bills, they could save up to 40 percent on their calls. Yet, the "Customer Guide" section in the front of the telephone book, which is supposed to provide you with full information on telephone service, doesn't even mention to consumers that they can get long-distance service from companies other than AT&T.

Over the years, most consumers do not seem to notice their telephone bill. It has seemed relatively small when compared to the costs of other basic essentials, such as food, energy, and housing. A $40 telephone bill can be seen as relief following a $250 electric bill or a $700 mortgage payment. However, these $30, $40, and $50 payments helped to form the financial backbone of the largest corporation in the world—the American Telephone and Telegraph Company.

Telephone service is going to change drastically for most consumers in the next few years. The most notable change is likely to be a doubling or tripling of their monthly phone bill. The breakup of AT&T already has fostered a host of new and complex proposals to change the way telephone service will be offered and billed to consumers. Framed generally as merely restructuring of rates, these changes are likely to result in an immediate and drastic increase in the cost of telephone service to the average American.

It is not likely that telephone service will be taken for granted any longer.

Reverse the Charges is an important starting point for those consumers who want to fight back. It includes dozens of money-saving tips that consumers can use to cut monthly phone bills for years to come.

Reverse the Charges also can help the interested consumer to understand the changes that are taking place within the telephone industry, especially now that AT&T is splitting up. There are numerous proceedings taking place that will have important long-term implications for the quality and affordability of basic telephone services.

However, most consumers, both individually and in groups, do not have the resources to get involved in complex cases. Since 1974, I have advocated a permanent mechanism for consumer representation called the Residential Utility Consumer Action Group, or RUCAG. These statewide organizations are being proposed in several legislatures to allow consumers to join together by checking a box on their monthly utility bill. By pooling consumer contributions of say $5 a year, a full-time group of skilled advocates, researchers, writers, and community organizers could be formed to defend utility consumer rights before the legislature, regulatory agencies, and the courts. A version of RUCAG, called the Citizens Utility Board (CUB), has been created in Wisconsin and is already at work. RUCAG bills have also passed one house of the legislatures in Maryland, New York, and California, but in each case the utilities blocked them in the other legislative house. The consumer movement will try again until success is achieved.

In the 1980s, consumers will be confronted by new telephone company impositions and restrictions that will add to existing complaints. It is clear, for example, that the telephone companies are determined to meter the frequency and duration of local calls, resulting in turning local calls into a long-distance type system. The trend toward great complexity in ratemaking and the associated technology to measure such detailed usage patterns will continue to produce higher telephone bills and increased user anxieties. Telephone utilities try to justify such tailoring of the rates to customer usage. Let each customer pay according to the use of the telephone, they say. This sounds defensible in principle, and in the short term some customers may receive a modest reduction in their monthly bills. But then the increased costs of complex usage-measuring equipment and complex billing practices will take its toll on customers, no matter what their usage may be. Moreover, consumers have no way of independently verifying message units and other indices of micro-usage, nor do the state utility commissions at present. The computer becomes both the master and trustee in the company's drive for maximum profit from minimum flat-rate service. More consumer attention is likely to be diverted toward these billing struggles and away from broader issues of liberating new technologies from the roadblocks of AT&T to provide cheaper, more accessible telecommunications services in a competitive environment for millions of Americans. This is why there is such a compelling need for CUB-type consumer organizations that could link consumer members with their own full-time staff of advocates.

Readers who use this guide are invited to send descriptions of their experiences—both wins and losses—to the authors, c/o Telecommunications Research and Action Center, P.O. Box 12038, Washington, D.C. 20005. In this way, future editions of this publication will be even more useful.

— **Ralph Nader**

PHONE SERVICE–
IT'S A NEW DEAL

"The Telephone Company."

Until recently, we've always thought of our telephone service as coming from that ever-present monopoly, "the telephone company." Whether we wanted to get new phone service, have our home wired for extensions, or place a long-distance call, our natural inclination was to call "the telephone company." It's always seemed natural, as night follows day.

Up until a few short years ago, "the telephone company"—which to four of every five Americans meant American Telephone & Telegraph Company, or "Ma Bell"—was the sole source of all of the phone equipment and electronic phone connections that made up our nation's telephone service. To illustrate the peculiar nature of this system, it was as if the same company that provided electricity into our homes also required us to purchase all washing machines, toasters, clocks, radios, and other electrical appliances directly from them.

But then some enterprising souls got to thinking that they could do some things better than Ma Bell: they could make telephone equipment that was better or cheaper or more responsive to consumer needs, or could provide more economical long-distance calling services, and still make a profit.

It wasn't easy for these new competitors to get through the starting gate and into the marketplace. AT&T had a warm relationship of long standing with the Federal Communications Commission in Washington, D.C., which regulates long-distance service and certain technical and equipment standards for telephones. Local phone companies—the largest of them owned by AT&T—were also in the good graces of the public utility commissions and public service commissions in most states. The idea of phone service as a monopoly had deep historical roots; it had become institutionalized—as a "fact of life."

Competitors had their work cut out for them when they tried to convince regulators to open up the marketplace. The phone company controlled all of the relevant information about phone service, and somehow they always managed to make the threat of marketplace competition look treasonous. "Don't allow any outsiders to provide equipment or service to phone customers," the phone company executives would say. "It'll damage the integrity of the network." These ambiguous buzzwords— "integrity of the network"—provided effective protection against competition for many years.

During the 1950s and 1960s, there were many battles before the FCC, the state regulatory agencies, and the courts, all aimed at loosening up the phone company's stranglehold on service and equipment. For example, Ma Bell for years had prohibited consumers from attaching to its lines any device it had not supplied—again, the "integrity of the network" was at stake, claimed the company.

In 1975, after a decade of legal battles, the FCC finally confirmed the right of phone users to connect phones and other apparatus that they own (including answering machines and extension phones) to the basic telephone network, so long as the hookup caused no harm to anyone else's service. To assure that no "harm" would occur to the phone network's "integrity," the FCC established a program to approve equipment that met certain technical standards. As a result of that decision, dozens of companies jumped into the business of making telephone equipment that consumers can buy and hook up for their own use, and a new retail business was born.

Other companies wanted to use radio waves to provide long-distance telephone service to business users. In disputes before the FCC and the U.S. Court of Appeals that began back in 1969 (and still have no end in sight), these companies slowly but surely established their rights to provide competitive long-distance services using microwaves, which, simply put, are beams of energy bounced all around the nation between those large dishes you often see on top of buildings or antenna towers. These new companies at first were interested in serving only business users; now they also serve residential phone users and are expanding their services all the time.

During the past few years, the FCC has made a number of decisions that it hopes will further encourage competition in the telephone equipment and service markets. Congress, through several so-far-futile efforts to update the present federal communications laws (most of which were established in 1934, long before the use of satellites, microwaves, and computer technology), has clearly signaled that increased competition is the governing policy for the future. And with the recent settlement of the seven-year-old government antitrust suit against AT&T by the U.S. Department of Justice, competition has gained irresistible momentum.

So, what does all of this legal business mean to you, the phone consumer?

Simply, it means that the days of monopoly telephone service are gone forever. Once, it was possible to satisfy all of your telephone needs with one call to an AT&T business office. Phone style and color and the type of local service were requested, and an installer would appear at your door in a few days to install the phones. A single bill came each month, but it rarely told you more than the fact that a monthly charge was assessed for "service and equipment."

Although your local phone company (whether it is owned by AT&T, General Telephone, or some other company) may still hold a monopoly on the phone wire coming into your home, there is a whole new marketplace of products you can now hook up to that phone line and services you can acquire through that line. Subscribing to telephone service is now going to be much more like subscribing to electrical service. Although your local phone company will primarily provide you with dial tone service, the rest is going to be up to you.

Shopping for phone service and equipment is now like shopping for any other household appliance: you can pick and choose what best suits your needs and your pocketbook. You can now decide where to obtain your telephone—and whether you want to buy it or rent it. And you can shop around for the best equipment at the lowest price—with as many or as few features as you want, in styles to suit any taste or decor.

You can choose from among several different companies that offer long-distance telephone service, with more companies entering the market all the time. And, depending upon your family's calling habits, you can save up to half on what you usually pay for long-distance calls each month.

This increase in competition has been accompanied by a growing awareness on the part of consumers of their rights and the phone company's responsibilities. Even though your local phone company still holds a monopoly over parts of the telephone network, consumers and their advocates have worked to make phone companies live up to their responsibilities. For example, many local phone companies have been under pressure to give their customers more detailed information on monthly bills, so that consumers can know precisely what they're paying for and can decide whether they really need it. This has resulted in a complete redesign of the customer bill by AT&T. The company has strongly recommended that its regional operating companies* adopt the new billing format, so chances are you'll get a thorough breakdown of your service charges at least once a year.

Growing competition and growing consumer awareness should mean that your potential for getting good, efficient phone service at reasonable rates is better than ever. It's a new deal!

But changes in communications policy are happening so fast that it may be difficult to know just what all of these changes will mean for the typical consumer. The FCC decided in 1980 that AT&T must begin marketing its phone equipment through a separate subsidiary, effective January 1983. The AT&T/Justice Department settlement, approved on August 24, 1982, requires AT&T to divest itself of its 22 regional operating companies, and requires these new independent companies to provide access to customers in their service area for all competitive long-distance companies on an equal basis.

In short, the telephone business is not standing still, and neither are we. In this edition of *Reverse the Charges,* we've pulled together all the latest information you need on buying versus renting your phone, on choosing your local phone service, on selecting among competitive long-distance services, and on your rights as a telephone consumer. We've also included details on how you can get your telephone complaints resolved quickly and effectively, and on ways consumers can join together to help keep phone rates low and the quality of service high. Plus, we've provided an explanation of how the many legislative, judicial, and regulatory changes that have recently occurred or soon will occur may change the nature of your phone service. Also in this edition are detailed descriptions of new telephone equipment, custom-calling services, ways to place international long-distance calls, and the rise of "resellers," a new group of competitors in domestic long-distance services.

With all of this information in hand, you'll be the kind of smart phone consumer who's ready to benefit from the new era of competitive telecommunications. You will be able to choose the equipment and services that best suit your needs—and save money, too.

----

* Local phone companies—such as Pacific Telephone, New York Telephone, Illinois Bell, and Chesapeake & Potomac Telephone—are also known in the industry as "operating companies." We'll use these two terms interchangeably throughout this book.

YOUR BASIC SERVICE AND EQUIPMENT

In this section, we'll explain the changing nature of phone services provided by your local phone company and review the wide variety of phone equipment currently available from your local operating company and its competitors. As you read through these pages, there's one important principle you should keep in mind: Basic telephone service is now considered a necessity by most Americans; many states even include phone service in their public-assistance programs. But phone service and equipment, like any other consumer goods, can be basic or gold-plated. You should consider what you're paying for in phone service and equipment charges and ask yourself, "Do I really need this? Am I really getting the best possible deal with my current assortment of phone services and accessories?" Think first about what your needs are. Consider what you really want from your telephone, and ask yourself if you're getting your money's worth. Then put together the package of equipment and services that best suits your requirements, picking and choosing from the range now available from an ever-increasing number of providers.

Monthly Service Charges

One of the easiest ways to keep under control your telephone costs is to know exactly what you're paying for in the service and equipment charge that appears in your monthly bill, whether you're getting everything you're paying for, and whether you want and need those items.

The service and equipment charge normally consists of the monthly fee for basic telephone service (the right to get on the telephone line and into the worldwide phone network—what's known as the dial tone), the charges for rental of equipment from the phone company, plus other incidental charges. Your basic phone service rate may also include either unlimited calls within a specified geographical area or a call allowance (calls up to a specified dollar value) for calls within your local area. The bill may show a single item—"service and equipment"—without itemizing those charges.

Because many people do not know what their service and equipment charge includes, they may be paying for unwanted or unneeded service or hardware. It's even possible they're paying for services they are no longer receiving, or equipment they are no longer using.

It is simple to find out what services and equipment are included in your monthly charge, how much each item costs, and what you can eliminate or change in order to save money.

Many local operating companies send their customers an annual summary of all services and equipment, and the cost for each. In New York and Michigan, for example, this annual itemization is required by state law. It is also required in some parts of the service areas of Northwestern Bell, Southern Bell, and Pennsylvania Bell. The Chesapeake and Potomac (C&P) Telephone Company, which serves Maryland, Virginia, and the District of Columbia, also has initiated an annual cost breakdown. AT&T has recommended that all of its operating companies provide this service to their customers, but there is no uniform national policy.

If you haven't received an annual itemization yet, there's no need to sit around and wait to find out what you're paying for. You're entitled to know *now,* and the business office of your local phone company is there to tell you. (You'll find the phone number located in the "Customer Guide" at the front of your local White Pages directory.) Call the business office and ask them what's included in your monthly bill and how much they charge you for each item. If you don't understand what a particular item on your bill means, ask for an explanation.

The charts on the following pages list monthly charges for telephone services and equipment for eight metropolitan areas around the U.S. It will give you an idea of the categories of charges you'll want to know about.

RATES FOR LOCAL PHONE SERVICE*

Atlanta	Boston
Standard rotary line........$13.70	Standard rotary line.......$10.80
Standard Touch-Tone® line..14.70	Standard Touch-Tone line....11.40
Standard rotary phone........1.20	Standard rotary phone........1.10
Standard Touch-Tone phone..1.95	Standard Touch-Tone phone..1.95
Princess® rotary.............2.75	Princess rotary...............2.35
Princess Touch-Tone........3.50	Princess Touch-Tone........3.00
Trimline® rotary............3.00	Trimline rotary..............2.70
Trimline Touch-Tone........3.75	Trimline Touch-Tone........3.40
Extension service: same price as each phone	Extension service: same price as each phone
Nonpublished number........1.75	Nonpublished number.......1.45

* These rates were in effect in January 1983. The rates shown may not be representative of what you are paying. AT&T tells us, for example, that New York City's rates are the highest in the nation. Moreover, just before publication of this edition, New York Telephone filed for an $878-million rate increase, which, if granted, may substantially increase the cost of these items. Over $6 billion in rate-increase requests were either pending or planned by operating companies as of September 1982.

Note that these charges are for *rentals* of telephone equipment. In the past, AT&T's operating companies have not offered these popular phones for sale directly to consumers. But AT&T has recently proposed a plan to the Federal Communications Commission under which it will be permitted to offer for sale to all consumers the basic telephone equipment now in their homes. If accepted, the plan will not go into effect until January 1, 1984. In the meantime, however, eight states—New York, California, North Dakota, South Carolina, Pennsylvania, Maryland, Arizona, and Oregon—have proceeded to authorize the sale of telephones to consumers. Other "decorator" telephones can be purchased from the PhoneCenter Stores operated by AT&T. AT&T has also begun to sell its equipment through Sears retail outlets. And a wide variety of phones are available from competing retailers. See "Can You Really Own Your Own Phone?" in this book.

Chicago

Standard rotary line.......$11.00*
Standard Touch-Tone line...11.00*
Standard rotary phone........1.10
Standard Touch-Tone phone..2.55
Princess rotary...............2.85
Princess Touch-Tone.........4.60
Trimline rotary...............3.00
Trimline Touch-Tone.........4.75
Extension service:
      wire & jack..........20.50
Nonpublished number........1.50
* For 200 calls within city

New York

Standard rotary line.........$7.54
Standard Touch-Tone line.....9.71
Standard rotary phone........3.03
Standard Touch-Tone phone..3.73
Princess rotary...............5.65
Princess Touch-Tone.........6.78
Trimline rotary...............6.81
Trimline Touch-Tone.........8.16
Extension service: same price
      as each phone plus 78¢
Nonpublished number........1.49

Dallas

Standard rotary line........$12.65
Standard Touch-Tone line....13.90
Standard rotary phone........1.25
Standard Touch-Tone phone..1.80
Princess rotary...............2.50
Princess Touch-Tone.........3.40
Trimline rotary...............2.90
Trimline Touch-Tone.........3.60
Extension service: same price
      as each phone
Nonpublished number........1.05

Washington, D.C.

Standard rotary line.........$8.83
Standard Touch-Tone line.....9.59
Standard rotary phone........1.50
Standard Touch-Tone phone..2.71
Princess rotary...............2.76
Princess Touch-Tone.........3.51
Trimline rotary...............3.01
Trimline Touch-Tone.........4.01
Extension service: same price
      as each phone
Nonpublished number.........60¢

Los Angeles

Standard rotary line.........$7.00
Standard Touch-Tone line.....8.20
Standard rotary phone........1.00
Standard Touch-Tone phone..1.55
Princess rotary...............2.10
Princess Touch-Tone.........2.90
Trimline rotary...............2.50
Trimline Touch-Tone.........3.25
Extension service: 1 jack connection
      charge only
Nonpublished number.........15¢

San Francisco

Standard rotary line.........$7.00
Standard Touch-Tone line.....8.20
Standard rotary phone........1.00
Standard Touch-Tone phone..1.55
Princess rotary...............2.10
Princess Touch-Tone.........2.90
Trimline rotary...............2.50
Trimline Touch-Tone.........3.25
Extension service: same price
      as each phone
Nonpublished number.........15¢

You may have additional items included in your service and equipment charge, including special consumer services (such as "custom calling," described elsewhere in this chapter) to which you may subscribe.

Now that you know what the local operating company is billing you for:

• Make sure you actually have been getting all of these services. If you do not have equipment for which you have been paying, or if you have not been receiving a particular service for which you've been billed, you should report this to the business office of the local operating company and receive a refund of all monies erroneously paid.

• Consider the prices for different types of equipment. Rotary-dial telephones (the kind where you place your finger in the holes and dial) are cheaper to rent than Touch-Tone (push-button) telephones. The "standard" telephone set is cheaper than the Princess or Trimline phone. Buying your phone may be cheaper than renting it (more on that later).

• Consider extension phones. Are they useful enough to continue paying a monthly rental for? If you need extensions, would it be better to buy your own? You may be able to save money if you have fewer telephones but install additional jacks around the house so you can move the phone from place to place. (In most states, these jacks have to be installed by the phone company, and there is generally a one-time installation charge if you don't already have them. But this, too, is changing, and you may be able to purchase and install your own jack.) Or you could buy a so-called cordless phone with a built-in radio transmitter that allows you to walk around your house or yard and place and receive phone calls without wires.

The Best Service for You

You probably are entitled to choose from two or more monthly rate plans for local telephone service. Your local phone company may not take great pains to promote these money-saving plans, but they are rather easy to find out about. The traditional "flat-rate" option, in which you pay a substantial monthly fee, combines the "access charge" (the dial tone that hooks you into the telephone network) and the right to make an unlimited number of calls within your local service area at no additional charge. Flat-rate service remains the most popular among consumers: almost nine out of ten residential phone users pay flat rates.

In areas where "message rate service" is offered, consumers may choose between paying a flat rate, or paying for local calls based upon the total number of calls per month. The options include paying a small fee for the access charge, plus a separate charge for *each* local call (this service can have any of a number of names: "budget service," "lifeline rates," "economy service," or "low-use service"). Or you may choose to pay a slightly higher monthly access charge and receive an allowance of a limited number of local calls at no extra cost, with a separate charge for each local call beyond that allowance (this is often called "message unit" or "message rate" service).*

You should do some simple figuring to determine which local service available in your area is best for you. (This comparison is more difficult in areas with LMS, as we'll discuss later.) Frequently, consumers don't realize that their calling habits may make it cheaper for them to take a budget service. Several years ago, *Consumer Reports* magazine quoted a staff member of the California Public Utilities Commission who observed that 40 percent of the people in that state who were paying for "unlimited" (i.e., flat-rate) calling service would save money if they took a lower rate with a limited number of calls per month.

Here's an example of how you can figure out whether you're better off with flat-rate service or a message rate or economy alternative.

We took the basic rate information appearing in the "Customer Guide" pages in the front of the Washington, D.C., White Pages and made these comparisons:

---

* In many parts of the country, local phone companies are experimenting with yet another rate formula: "local measured service" (LMS), or "usage sensitive pricing" (USP). Under LMS, your local calls are billed according to any or all of several variables: the number of local calls you make, the amount of time you're on the line, the time of day your call is placed, and the distance between you and the party you're calling. You also pay an access charge at a reduced rate. Where LMS has been introduced, the phone company usually offers a limited option: take flat-rate service at a premium rate, or opt for LMS. (More on LMS later in this chapter.)

Type of Service	Monthly Rate	
	Rotary	Touch-Tone
Unlimited (flat rate): No limit to the number of calls in Washington, D.C., and its suburbs	$8.83	$9.59
Measured (actually "message rate"): An allowance of up to 60 local calls per month in Washington and suburbs; each call over 60 billed at 4.9 cents per call	4.51	5.27
D.C. rate: unlimited calls within Washington; calls to Maryland and Virginia suburbs billed at 4.9 cents per call	4.51	5.27
Economy rate: each local call (to Washington or suburbs) billed at 4.9 cents per call	2.20	2.96

When one of our researchers spoke with a local phone company service representative in Washington, she was warned that the economy rate is a wise choice only if you "almost never" use the phone. But a little simple arithmetic shows just how much you can use the phone and still save with the lowest rate plan:

Type of Service	Rotary	Touch-Tone
Most expensive monthly rate ("unlimited")	$8.83	$9.59
Lowest monthly rate ("economy")	2.20	2.96
Difference between highest and lowest monthly rates	$6.63	$6.63

If you divide the difference ($6.63) by the standard cost-per-call for economy-rate subscribers (4.9 cents each), you'll find that you'd need to make 135 local calls per month before the charge for economy service will equal that for unlimited service.

That means you could average more than four local calls every day and still save money with the economy rate. Remember, any long-distance calls you make over Bell's long-distance lines won't be counted against your monthly allowance. But any long-distance calls you make over competitive long-distance services—which we'll discuss in a minute—will be counted against the monthly allowance, since you must make a local call to "access" the long-distance company's computer. Incoming calls are not counted against your monthly allowance.

So once you've made a similar comparison of the various rates offered by *your* local phone company, how do you know which service is for you? Try this: Keep track of your personal calling habits for a month or two (you don't have to write down the numbers, just note if it's a local or a long-distance call). Once you know approximately how many local calls you make during a month, you'll be able to decide which service will cost you the least.

Some local phone companies keep track of the number of local calls you make each month and include that information on your bill; in that case, you have all the information you need to decide already at your fingertips. If not, and you want to figure it out yourself, it's important to know what is considered a local call by your phone company. A map or chart should appear in the "Customer Guide" at the front of your phone book indicating which telephone exchanges are within your local calling area. These exchanges are indicated by the three-digit prefix of the phone number you're calling. In some cases, there may be "extended area service" that results in a call being free going in one direction but incurring a toll when it goes the opposite way. That is, a friend in town B may be able to call you in town A for free, because town A is within town B's local service area. But you may be charged a toll when you call from town A to town B because the extended area service is only one way. Answers to such questions about one-way extended service should be provided clearly in the front of your phone book—but if you have a question, you should call the operator or your local telephone business office. (*Don't* call Directory Assistance for rate questions. Directory Assistance operators don't have that data, and you will be charged for an information call if that service isn't free in your area.)

If you are moving into a new area, you may not yet know what your calling habits will be like or how many local calls you are likely to make. You will have to choose the type of service you want when you first move in, without an opportunity to review the way you make calls. It's possible that later you will want to change from one type of service to another. You should ask your telephone business office or service representative about the cost of switching from one service to another at a later time. If there is no charge, no problem. But in many states there is a charge whether you move from a more expensive to a less expensive service or vice versa. In a few states there is no charge when you go from a more expensive service to a less expensive one. In that case, it might be a good idea to start with a higher monthly service and move down to less expensive service as your calling habits are more clearly established. In some states you may change your service without charge for a certain period of time—sixty days, say—after a rate hike has been approved. You should receive notification of this charge-free period with your phone bill, so take a look at any inserts you receive.

Custom Calling

In addition to choosing your local calling service rate, you may want to consider another group of services available from your local phone company. "Custom calling" is offered by AT&T's local operating companies in many areas. Here's a summary of custom calling services as prepared by an AT&T representative:

- **Call waiting:** If you are talking on the phone and someone else is trying to call you, a tone tells you that another call is waiting. You can put the first party on hold and answer the second call. This can be a cheaper alternative to getting a second phone line.

- **Call forwarding:** This option allows you to have your calls forwarded to another number, either to be answered by you when you are at a location other than your home or to be answered by someone else for you when you are away. This can provide an alternative to a remote-control answering machine, and can assure timely notice of calls received. It may also provide extra security when you are away from home.

- **Three-way calling:** This option allows you to hold a conversation with two parties at the same time. Example: Without three-way calling, Sue calls Mary to meet with her and Joan (call #1); Mary suggests a meeting time and place to Sue, and Sue must check back with Joan to see if it's OK (call #2); Joan tells Sue it's OK, Sue calls Mary back to confirm (call

#3). With three-way calling: Sue could call Mary (call #1), and Sue would then add Joan on (call #2), saving one call. This can save callers some money, especially where local measured service is in effect. It's also a lot less frustrating for Joan, Mary, and Sue.

- **Speed calling:** This is a convenience that allows you to set up a series of one- or two-digit codes in place of seven-digit local phone numbers or ten-digit long-distance numbers that you dial frequently. Joan is president of the local PTA. She calls her ten-person board of directors several times a week. Joan can code all ten numbers into the system and "dial" merely by punching the code number, e.g., #4, #5, etc.

These features are available for monthly charges, and there may be a discount if bought in certain combinations. (Note: these features are a function of the local switching office of your phone company, not a function of equipment in your home.) You should check with your local phone company's business office to determine availability in your area.

Smart telephone shoppers will investigate alternatives to custom calling which may be less expensive in the long run. Custom calling services are charged on a monthly basis, with rates as high as $4 to $7 each month for some or all of the services. There are a growing number of telephone accessories available for purchase and easy hook-up to your home telephone that perform many of the same functions as custom calling services. For example, a portable automatic dialer capable of storing up to nine sixteen-digit numbers sells for only $35. Speed calling service from the telephone company for eight numbers, which can be used only from a subscriber's home, costs, in Washington, D.C., $1.50 per month, or $18 per year. The portable automatic dialer thus pays for itself, compared to the telephone company speed calling, in two years.

Local Measured Service

Phone consumers around the nation are increasingly likely to hear about "local measured service" (LMS) being implemented in their areas, and it's likely to be the center of some controversy.

In theory, LMS works like this:

As consumer and business usage increases, the phone company has to build more lines and install more phone equipment. Those who use the phone most often, especially during peak hours (when the demand on the phone network is the greatest), theoretically are most responsible for the additional costs incurred by the phone company. LMS is intended to place the cost of phone usage on those imposing the cost.

In practice, here's how LMS works: Every time you place a local phone call, you are billed in a way that's similar to the way long-distance calls are billed. That is, you may be billed for the number of calls you make, the time of day you call, the amount of time you're on the line, and the distance between you and the party you're calling. In New York, all four variables are calculated into the billing. In other areas, only one or two variables are taken into account ("message rate" service is an example—you are billed according to the number of local calls you make).

In some ways, LMS should make it easier for you to control your telephone costs. You will want to call during off-peak hours in order to be charged lower rates. And you will want to keep calls shorter, for additional savings.

But in practice, LMS pricing schemes can be very complex. A consumer attempting to make a reasoned choice between flat-rate service and LMS faces mind-boggling calculations. Moreover, many consumer advocates have challenged LMS rate schemes as arbitrary and not truly based on cost.

Nevertheless, LMS has begun to establish itself in many parts of the country and is likely to spread. Your local phone company should be in a position to assist you in choosing between flat-rate and LMS. Many telephone companies are starting to offer a free trial period for LMS, during which you can switch to LMS for a time to compare costs, and then switch back to flat-rate service (if you so choose) without incurring an additional charge. AT&T's local operating companies have attempted to promote LMS by offering this "free look" idea.

There's another way local phone companies can assist consumers in comparing flat-rate and LMS: by providing "parallel billing." This means the local phone company sends the consumer a bill charging LMS rates for the services used during the month, and another bill showing what the same services would have cost under the flat-rate plan. This allows a real head-to-head comparison of rates, but requires that the consumer pay careful attention to his or her calling habits in order to achieve additional savings. Most local operating companies have been very reluctant to offer parallel billing.

If your local phone company offers parallel billing or a free look, you should take advantage of it. If these informational services are not offered, you should urge your phone company to do so, or urge your state regulatory commission to require it.

Should You Pay a Deposit?

Like every other business, the phone company likes people with good credit records. But sometimes, regardless of your financial history, the phone company may ask for a deposit in order to assure they'll receive your payments regularly.

The phone company's decision on whether to require a deposit is probably most heavily influenced by your prior credit experience with them. If you have had previous telephone service for a year or more, do not owe the telephone company any money, and were never temporarily denied service for not paying your bill, a deposit will not be required.

If you've had no prior telephone experience, the service representative will ask you a series of six to ten credit questions. Typical questions include:

- Have you worked two years or more at your present job?
- Do you have a savings account?
- Do you have a checking account?
- Have you any current loans outstanding?
- Do you own your home?
- Do you have a major credit card?
- Do you have an oil company credit card?
- Do you have any other credit card?
- Do you own a motor vehicle?
- Are you over fifty years of age?

The more yes answers you are able to give, the better your credit picture (as far as the phone company is concerned) and the less likely you are to have to pay a deposit. These questions make up a so-called "credit screen," which Bell requires its employees to apply uniformly and without asking for specifics. These factors were found in AT&T studies to be indicators of good credit risks.

Your phone company's credit policy has to pass approval by your state's public utility or public service commission. The company's credit policy will be outlined in the company's "tariff," or schedule of rates or charges. This tariff is on file with your state public utility or public service commission and must be made available by the phone company for your inspection.

The phone company is required to return your deposit within one year's time, and to pay you interest on the full amount. The sole exception to returning it within a year is if you were temporarily denied service for non-payment during that twelve-month period—and the phone company can only temporarily deny you service after it has followed certain procedures. If there are other circumstances, you may ask the phone company to take these into account when that year rolls around.

The interest rate paid on deposits varies from state to state, but currently ranges from 5 to 9 percent simple interest per year. You are entitled to know the rate of interest your deposit will earn.

If you have a good service record, you may ask the phone company to review your credit status in advance of the end of one year in order to receive a refund of your deposit.

If you feel the credit screen has been applied unfairly, or if you have any other difficulties with the phone company service representative over your deposit, remember that for every five Bell employees there is a supervisor. Simply say, "I want to speak with your supervisor on this matter."

Choosing Your Phone Equipment

When you talk to the phone company's service representative about what sort of equipment you should get, remember this: he or she wants to separate you from your money. After all, the service representative is really a salesperson and is rewarded by the phone company for making sales.

The representative may try to persuade you to buy more equipment than you need or to buy unneeded extra service. Service representatives are supposed to help you analyze your phone needs and recommend the most appropriate service, but some are likely to try to downplay the desirability of cheaper services and equipment, and instead push more expensive options. (Some people charge that the phone company *requires* its employees to push these higher-priced options.) Sometimes the service representative won't tell you about some of the lower-priced options even though he or she is supposed to do so—laws in many states now require them to inform you of all the alternatives.

A prime example of this behavior is the service representative who quotes you the price for Touch-Tone (push-button dialing) as if it were the standard or normal price, when in fact rotary dial service is less expensive than Touch-Tone. (And with so-called "universal dial" telephones available from many manufacturers, you can have some of the convenience of push-button dialing at rotary dial rates; more on this later.)

If you feel that you're being pressured by the service representative or that the representative isn't really helping you figure out your phone needs,

speak with another one, or with a supervisor. Be firm, and don't be forced
into buying extras that you do not want. It pays to ask very direct questions; otherwise you run the risk of getting incomplete information, as staff
members of the New York City Department of Consumer Affairs discovered
when they posed as phone customers and called 17 different business offices for information on phone service. Not one willingly gave them all the
information they requested.

   You should be aware of the fact that *you are not required to rent or buy
any of your telephone equipment from the local telephone company as a
condition for receiving phone service.* It is perfectly legal for you to obtain
your dial tone from the local telephone company while you rent or buy your
phone equipment from any source you choose, just as long as the equipment is FCC-approved. There are practical advantages and disadvantages
to getting your equipment from the phone company, which we will set out
below.

   When you begin your telephone service, the phone company will bill
you for a "service connection" charge. This is intended to cover the phone
company's actual cost of providing you with a dial tone, adding you to the
telephone network, and listing you in Directory Assistance and the telephone
book. You'll have to pay a service connection charge no matter who provides your telephone equipment. If the phone company provides the equipment, there will also probably be a service charge if a phone company installer comes out to your home, and an installation charge if the installer
actually has to perform any labor besides plugging your new phone into
a jack in the wall.

   There are ways to reduce these charges. If you're willing to use the phone
equipment and extension jacks left behind by a previous occupant, there
will be no service or installation charges. (If you don't like what's already
in, the phone company must take any and all of it out at your request for
free.) If your new home is already equipped with telephone-company-
installed jacks for new phones, you can save money by bringing your old
telephone with you and plugging it in yourself. (If your new home has old-
fashioned jacks, however—the four-pronged kind or the ones where you
need a screwdriver to hook up your phone—it might be necessary to have
a phone company installer pay a visit to your home to make some changes.
More about jacks and plugs later.)

   There are some other options. AT&T's shops, called PhoneCenter Stores,
offer new phones for sale. Local telephone company Service Center stores
rent telephones (and repair phones purchased prior to January 1, 1983).

In either case, you can pick up the phones you want to rent or buy along with your phone books and any other equipment you may need, again saving the charge of an installer's visit.

You can even purchase your own phone from any of a number of suppliers other than the phone company—and therein lies a tale.

Can You Really Own Your Phone?

Up until 1981, you really couldn't buy *any* phone from the phone company. Although the phones appeared to be for sale, if you "bought" one, all you really owned was the *exterior* of the phone—the Mickey Mouse, Superman, or whatever form the plastic was molded into; the phone company owned the *interior*—all the electrical and mechanical parts that make the thing work. Legally, the phone belonged to them.

Now, all of that has changed. Beginning on January 1, 1983, Ma Bell, through a new wholly owned subsidiary called American Bell, began to sell all of its telephones, including the Princess® and Trimline® telephones. In most states you can buy these phones directly from your local PhoneCenter Store; as of January 1, 1983, you can also buy them at Sears, now an authorized outlet for American Bell equipment. Both Sears and the PhoneCenter Stores offer warranties, just like most other retailers.

The growth of a small but thriving competitive retail phone-selling business is probably the most dramatic new development in the phone equipment industry. This new industry came about after years of legal controversy.

AT&T used to prohibit connection of non-Bell equipment to its lines. Fortunately, Bell lost consumer challenges to that monopoly. Then Bell tried to force consumers who wanted to use their own equipment to rent an adapter from Bell to safeguard the "integrity of the network." The adapters, of course, quickly ate up the cost advantages of owning your own phone. Thankfully, Ma Bell lost that battle, too.

It is now completely legal to purchase your own phone and install it in your home, thereby eliminating both the service and installation charges for a phone company installer and the monthly equipment rental charge. Anyone can install a phone, as long as they follow a few restrictions imposed by the Federal Communications Commission.

According to FCC rules, the equipment you install must meet FCC's technical criteria to make sure it doesn't harm the phone network. (Note that FCC approval does not necessarily assure the *quality* of the phone equipment.) Any piece of equipment you install should have an "FCC registration number" that indicates the equipment conforms to its technical standards. The phone also should be labeled with a "ringer equivalency number," which tells you how much electric current your phone's bell drains off the line; typically, this is a decimal number (1.0, for example), followed by the letter A or B. You must call your phone company's business office to tell them you are going to plug in the new phone, and read these two numbers to them. As soon as you have called, you may install the equipment. (Failure to notify the phone company about the equipment you install may lead to suspension of phone service, and may ultimately result in termination of service, although this action is rarely taken.) If you move the equipment or disconnect or reconnect it, you need not call the phone company each time.

If you have been paying a monthly rental to the phone company for use of their equipment, you should be sure to let them know if you choose to disconnect it so you will no longer be billed, and you should return the equipment to a Service Center.

If the phone equipment you buy does not have an FCC registration number, it still may be okay to use. If the equipment was legally connected to the phone system prior to July 1, 1979, then it does not need to have an FCC registration number. If you are not sure when your equipment was first connected, you may call the FCC (202-632-1833/35) for more information.

Another option is to have an equipment refurbisher inspect your phone to see whether it meets FCC standards. A list of FCC-registered refurbishers may be found at the back of this book. If you purchase a phone without an FCC registration number, you may bring it to one of these refurbishers for an inspection to see whether it meets government standards. If it does, the refurbisher will assign it a registration number. Similarly, if you are concerned or uncertain about any equipment you have purchased or found, a refurbisher will inspect and/or repair it to bring it up to government standards.

Keep in mind that phone equipment you purchase from sources other than the phone company may not be connected to any party line or a pay phone. Only private lines are covered by the FCC ruling allowing you to hook up your own phone equipment.

Plugs and Jacks

There are a few things to know about phone plugs and jacks, and how to wire your home for phone service.

While it is legal to own a phone, only thirty-one states currently allow consumers to do their own internal wiring—that is, any of the telephone wiring within your home (see box below); at this writing, consumers in at least ten other states are trying to get legal authority to do their own wiring.

CUSTOMER-INSTALLED WIRING STATES

Arizona	Massachusetts	Ohio (Cincinnati
California	Maryland	Bell only)
Connecticut	Minnesota	Oklahoma
Colorado	Mississippi	Oregon
Florida	Missouri	South Carolina
Georgia	Nevada	Tennessee
Idaho	New Hampshire	Texas
Illinois	New Jersey	Washington
Indiana	New York	West Virginia
Kansas	North Carolina	Wisconsin
Kentucky	North Dakota	

A number of local phone companies have implemented what they call Customer-Provided Inside Wiring (CPIW) programs to help residential customers install their own wiring. (New York Telephone, Pacific Telephone, and Illinois Bell have started these programs.) Under the CPIW program, consumers have the option of allowing the phone company to install the inside wiring, having a contractor install the wiring, or installing it themselves. The telephone company will maintain the customer-provided wire (for either a monthly or a per service visit charge) so long as the phone company standards are met. Along with the implementation of the CPIW programs, the phone company provides a line of do-it-yourself wiring kits.

It is not always easy to tell when you will save money by installing your own inside wiring. The rules are new and complex. Many telephone com-

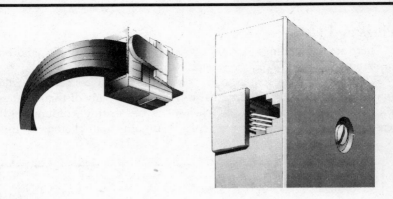

Figure 1—modular plug

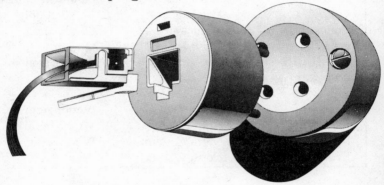

Figure 2—four-prong to modular adaptor

Figure 3—"T" adaptor

pany business representatives are not aware of the specific options available and the costs involved. As a result, it is difficult to get accurate and reliable information.

In New York, for example, it does make sense to wire your own extension telephone. New York Telephone charges $55.31 to come out and do the installation. But if you purchase the wire and a jack from the phone company, it will cost you only $12.90 to do it yourself ($6.95 for 50 feet of wire and $5.95 for a jack). You probably could do it for even less if you purchase the wire and jack from another source, such as a department store.

However, it may cost you more to wire your new home or apartment in New York than it does to have New York Telephone come out and do it for you. In New York City, the phone company will charge you $70.38 to wire a new home or apartment and install a new jack. If you were to try to do it yourself, it could cost as much as $76.

We found the same situation in other cities. The savings from wiring a new, unwired home or apartment is usually slight. The savings for installing extension telephones is usually great. But to be sure, call your business office and get the precise details on just what it will cost for the phone company to do the wiring for you. Remember, if the service representative you speak with cannot answer your questions, ask to speak to a supervisor.

If you cannot or do not wish to do your own wiring, you'll have to ask the phone company to install wires and plugs. For this service there is a one-time installation fee plus a service-call charge, but usually no additional monthly charge. But the rates for installation by the phone company are skyrocketing by as much as 200 percent. Under the recent FCC orders phone companies must charge you the entire cost of installation. Since these costs are likely to be substantial, you should ask about paying in installments. In New York, for example, you can spread payments over six months.

When the phone company installs its jacks, they use modular plugs—plugs that can be used by just about any phone, answering machine, automatic dialer, or other module. (See figure 1.) The four-pronged plug and jack that were once used by most phone companies are now obsolete.

If your home has the obsolete four-pronged variety of jacks and you wish to install a phone with the new modular type of plug, you may use an adapter to make them compatible. Adapters may be purchased from many telephone equipment stores, electronic equipment stores (such as Radio Shack), and many hardware and drug stores; sometimes they are even available from the phone company at no charge. There are two types of adapters: the four-prong to modular adapter (figure 2), which enables you to plug a modular phone plug into a four-pronged jack in the wall; and a "T adapter" (figure 3), which enables you to add an automatic dialer or an answering machine to your phone line without having to install extra hardware. Both adapters take only a few minutes to install.

With modular jacks and plugs, it's also easy to wire your own extension phone. Simply plug a "T adapter" (figure 3) into a modular jack, and insert a cord with a modular plug (figure 1) into the "T." Run a cord of the desired length along the base of your wall, carrying it up and around doors, flush against the woodwork. You may want to secure the cord carefully with a staple gun. Once you have brought the cord to the room where you want the extension, simply plug the end directly into a phone. Or you may want to terminate the cord at the baseboard and use a "cord coupler," which is a two-sided jack. One end hooks into the plug on the cord, and the other end is open to receive the cord from your extension phone. Cord couplers are available wherever phone accessories are sold.

One last consideration in buying your own phone equipment: If you have trouble with your phone service and must call in a phone company repairer to find the trouble, the problem had better not originate with your purchased equipment, or it could cost you plenty. If the repairer finds the phone equipment that you own is the culprit, you'll get a stiff bill from the phone company for the visit. The phone company is willing to repair your phone equipment, but it may cost you another $30 to $50 in repair costs. (Ma Bell reports that it is currently reviewing its policy of repairing non-Bell equipment.) Keep in mind that a reconditioned phone from the many non-Bell stores may cost you as little as $20, so these repair fees are hardly worth it.

In some cities, new central office equipment allows the phone company to determine electronically whether a problem originates in their lines or in your phone, without the need for a service call. But it doesn't hurt to take a few simple precautions before you call the phone company. First, check each instrument in your home individually by placing a call while each instrument is disconnected. Thus, if you have two phones and an answering machine, make a total of three calls: one with instrument number one disconnected, one with instrument number two disconnected, and one with instrument number three disconnected. If the problem is in one of the three instruments, it should disappear when the faulty machine is unplugged. If the problem persists after this test, then the trouble is likely either to be in your wiring (which the telephone company will maintain, even if you installed it yourself in those states with a CPIW program), or with telephone company equipment.

In any case, you are likely to save a great deal of money if instead of calling for a repairer to come to your home, you take any equipment you think is malfunctioning to a telephone company Service Center, if it is Western Electric, or to a local phone repair outlet if the equipment is from another company.

Tips on Shopping for Phone Equipment

These days you can buy your own phone from a great many different suppliers: drug and department stores, electronics shops, specialized telephone boutiques, even mail-order houses. Many of these outlets are listed under ''Telephone Equipment'' in the Yellow Pages.

When you buy a phone from one of these sources, you will own it—inside and out. So you'll want to make an intelligent selection, taking into account the cost of the instrument, its features, the warranty, and more.

Here is a checklist of things to do when shopping for a new phone:

- **Check the cover.** Is it smooth and well finished with no jagged edges? Cushions on the bottom of the phone help prevent scratching the surface it will rest on. The phone's cord should release smoothly without lifting the base off the table when you pick up the handset.
- **Ask for a demonstration.** Ask if you can use the equipment to call a friend—or the weather, or whatever. Is the sound clear? Does the person called hear you clearly? Try the dial or buttons; they should operate smoothly without sticking.
- **Make sure it's legal.** Check for an FCC registration number; it must have one for you legally to plug the phone into your home's system. Check that the ringer equivalency number is compatible with your phone system. The ringer equivalency number tells you the amount of current the phone uses when it rings. Wiring varies; if you exceed the number of phones, or if you use phones that drain off too much current, your phone may not ring.
- **Read the warranty.** Most new-phone warranties cover labor for 90 days and parts for one year. Refurbished phones may have substantially shorter warranty periods. Note whether the retailer provides warranty coverage that supplements the manufacturer's. Find out exactly what is covered and where you can get the phone fixed or replaced; with some phones, you must pack it up and send it across the country to the manufacturer's service facility. Find out if you can get a replacement phone while yours is in the shop.

- **Check the plug.** Try to get a phone with the same type of plug as you have in your home. Otherwise, you may also need an adapter.
- **Make sure it's suitable.** Know where you intend to use your phone and the type of use you'll make of it before you make your choice. A rotary-dial phone will not permit you to use a long-distance service unless you buy an adapter, for example. And neither the new electronic telephones nor the various lightweight phones available hold up well under heavy use. Some phones may echo and so may be difficult to use for long-distance calling. Don't get stuck with a phone that is perfectly good but that doesn't fit your needs. You don't save if you can't use it!
- **Shop around.** Phones with very similar features can have very different prices. For example, new electronic telephones such as the GTE ''Flip Phone'' or the Teleconcepts ''Gabbifone'' are available for under $50, while a Bell phone with similar features costs $79.95 at PhoneCenter Stores. In general, a basic new rotary phone will probably cost $25 to $30; a refurbished rotary phone should cost somewhat less. Designer phones, on the other hand, frequently cost well over $100.

  If you're looking for new telephones, there are a growing number of stores that specialize in and sell only telephones and accessories. Electronic stores and franchise outlets often carry a line of telephones and related equipment, and most drug and department stores are offering telephones for sale in their camera departments. In some cases, generous discounts off the list price may be available.

  If you're looking for used phones, consider government surplus sales, garage sales, and stores that sell used hardware and housing fixtures; with persistence, you may be able to pick up a bargain. But remember to check such phones for that all-important FCC registration number; if it's not there, you'll probably have to have the phone refurbished.
- **Don't automatically buy the phones in your home.** In most states, the local telephone company will be offering to sell you the phones that are already in your home by January 1, 1984. Before you accept the offer, be sure to take the time to find out whether buying existing phones is really a bargain. In New York State, for example, New York Telephone recently sold its standard rotary-dial phones to consumers for $35, considerably more than the $24.95 it costs for a new Stromberg-Carlson rotary desk phone, and almost as much as the $40 (approximately) that it costs to buy a refurbished ITT touch-type phone. And the warranty on Bell's in-home phones was good for only a month!

When you shop for your own phone, remember that the marketplace abounds with choices—not just in shapes and colors, but in gadgetry and convenience as well. Some examples:

• Telephone answering machines will take messages while you're away from home or unable to come to the phone. With some machines, you can call in for messages from virtually any phone in the world.

• Repertory or automatic dialers allow you to preprogram telephone numbers, and to dial these numbers by punching a single button. This can be particularly helpful if you use one of the non-Bell long-distance services, which require you to dial several access codes in addition to the number you're calling.

• Speaker phones allow you to talk with your hands free, and to let others in the room in on the conversation.

• Cordless phones allow you to carry your phone all around the house (and even just outside), unencumbered by a wire. A small radio transmitter links you with the base of your phone, which can be up to 300 feet away with some models.

• Some phones offer a mute that cuts off the speaker, but not the receiver; as a result, you can talk to someone else in the room, but the person at the other end of the line can't hear you. Other phones offer digital displays that time your calls or can be used as a calculator or clock; memory dialing that dials numbers repeatedly if they are busy; memories that store frequently called numbers; and hold buttons.

• And, of course, there are ''decorator'' phones in the shape of cartoon characters or beer cans, or in hand-painted porcelain, wooden chests, onyx sculptures, and just about any other material imaginable.

What Are You Likely to Save?

If you're buying your new phone to save money—and not just because it offers useful features or because you find it attractive or novel—you should first call your phone company's business office to determine whether your state's public utilities or public service commission has authorized your local phone company to reduce customers' bills by the amount they would otherwise pay for rental of a phone from the phone company.

The rental charges for phone company equipment can vary dramatically—from as little as 75 cents per month for a basic rotary (dial) phone in

Wyoming, to up to $8 per month for a Trimline Touch-Tone phone in New York.

Some states do not yet allow for a discount in your monthly phone bill when you provide your own phone equipment. But in most states the savings range from 50 cents to $3 per month per phone. If you add up the savings over two or three years, you'll probably save enough to pay back the cost of the phone you bought. For example, if you purchase a phone for $35, and you save $3 per month by not renting your phone from the phone company, that $35 purchase price will pay itself back in reduced costs in less than a year. After that, you pocket all of the extra savings.

And those savings should continue for a while. Telephones have a reasonably long life span of reliable service. AT&T executives estimate that their phones require servicing no more than *once every seven years,* and that the average telephone lasts ten years with two overhauls during the time it's in use. (If you save $1.50 a month for ten years, that's $180 in savings—more than enough to have your phone overhauled, or even to have it replaced.) Staffers at the FCC report that the life expectancy for most other FCC-registered phones manufactured by AT&T's competitors is roughly the same as for Bell equipment. (But remember: FCC registration does not necessarily certify the phone's quality; it only means that the phone is compatible with the national phone network.)

If you want or need push-button telephone service, there are ways to get the convenience without the cost.

"Universal dial" phones offer the convenience of push-button dialing without requiring you to pay the additional monthly fee for Touch-Tone service. Universal-dial phones have a pad of numbers, like any push-button phone. But the universal-dial phone is compatible with rotary (dial) lines as well as Touch-Tone lines. When you push the buttons of a universal-dial phone, the phone sends pulses down the wire, rather than the tones you hear when you dial with a Touch-Tone phone. So, you get the convenience of push-button dialing without the cost.

Universal-dial phones may not be usable with some of the services that require Touch-Tone service, such as banking-by-phone services or making long-distance calls using one of the new competitive services. But for these types of service, you may need only an electronic "touch pad." The touch pad is a small electronic converter that generates the tones that make Touch-Tone service work. One such converter on the market is called the "Soft Touch," which sells for about $25. It is placed in the mouthpiece of your phone receiver and you simply punch in your tones. There are several others on the market at similar prices.

How to Save on Local and In-State Calls*

You've chosen the monthly rate that's most economical for you and decided on your equipment needs. Your basic phone system is now in place. How can you save money when you use it?

Let's look first at directory assistance, or "information," as it's often called. You've undoubtedly heard about the phone company's campaign to get you to "use the book" to find phone numbers rather than to call the directory assistance (DA) operator. That's good advice. Up until recently you may not have thought twice about calling DA. But the phone company has convinced most state regulatory commissions that DA costs are too high, and that the phone company should be allowed to pass along those high costs to those who make DA calls. In most cases, the regulatory agencies have given phone companies permission to charge for at least some DA calls.

The system for billing DA calls varies from state to state. Usually, you are given a monthly allowance of free DA calls; any calls over that monthly allowance will cost you, typically 10 to 30 cents each. Such charges may be levied for requests for phone numbers in your state; requests for numbers of those who are not listed in the phone book; requests for area code information from DA (area code information is always free if you dial Operator—"0").

On the other hand, there is usually no charge for DA calls made from hotel and motel guest rooms, club phones, hospital phones, and mobile phones. And there is never a charge for calls to DA in other states, or calls to DA made from pay phones.

If you are visually or physically disabled or certified as unable to use the telephone directory, you will not be charged for DA calls. Contact your phone company's business office for details.

If you call the DA operator for assistance and are given a wrong number, you should not be charged for the DA call. Call DA back for the correct number and let the DA operator know that the number you were given was wrong. You should not be charged for the second DA call—hopefully, for the *right* number. And, of course, if the wrong number you were given required you to make a long-distance call, you should call the operator to get credit for the call.

---

* We use the traditional terminology in this book to refer to calls within a state—"intrastate"—and calls made to another state—"interstate." With changes taking place in regulations and with the break-up of AT&T, this terminology is changing. You will be hearing increasingly the term "interexchange" in reference to all toll calls between two different city exchanges, and "intraexchange" to describe what is now called a local call.

The phone company provides directories—phone books—at no charge
for areas within your state that you frequently call. Contact the business
office and ask to have the directories sent to you. You also may obtain out-
of-state directories from your local phone company. There may be a han-
dling charge. Directories for many areas are usually found in public libraries
and in your local phone company business office.

You may use toll-free "800" and "Enterprise" numbers to save money
when you call businesses. The 800 numbers, also known as WATS (for
"Wide Area Telephone Service") lines, are a way for many companies to
allow customers to call them toll free. Although the phone company does
not publish a directory of 800 numbers, you may find out whether such
a number exists for any company by calling WATS information:
800-555-1212. Enterprise numbers are another way to provide local access
to businesses located far away. You make an Enterprise call by dialing
Operator and asking for the number. There is no charge for such calls.

You may locate area codes in the front of your telephone book. If you
can't determine the area code for a particular city, dial Operator for information; *don't* call Directory Assistance, or you may be charged for the
information.

You probably already know that you can save money on toll calls by taking advantage of "time-of-day" discounts, which generally are in effect between 5 PM and 8 AM, and all day Saturday, Sunday, and holidays. At certain times the discounts are greater than at others; your phone directory
can provide this information.

You may not know that there are "toll discount plans" in effect in 15
states that can save money on intrastate (in-state) toll calls. These plans are
often underpublicized, and their details change frequently. If there is one
in your state, and if your calling habits coincide with the plans' requirements,
you could save substantially. Here is a sampling of the types of plans in
effect at the time we went to press (for complete details, call your phone
company's business office):

- In **Minnesota**, the "Gopher State Plan" allows you to make a ten-minute
  call anywhere within the state for $1.65 between 5 PM and 11 PM Mon-
  day through Friday, or Saturday and Sunday between 8 AM and 11 PM.
  You may also make a twenty-minute call for $1.65 any night between
  11 PM and 8 AM. Each additional minute costs 8 cents. These rates are
  applied to your calls automatically if you live in Minnesota—you don't
  have to make any special arrangements.

- Both **Oregon** and **Washington** have "ten minutes for a dollar" plans for in-state toll calls. In Oregon, the special rate applies between 10 PM and 8 AM. In Washington, it applies on weekdays from 10 PM to 8 AM, on Saturdays from 8 AM to 10 PM, and on Sundays from 8 AM to 5 PM. These rates also are automatic—you need no special arrangements.
- In **New York,** you can obtain "Dial-A-Visit" service from New York Bell. For a minimum monthly charge of $5, you get a discount of up to 40 percent on your toll calls within New York State if you dial direct (without operator assistance) between 5 PM and 8 AM on weekdays, or anytime on weekends.
- **Wisconsin** offers a similar program called "Tele-Visit." Two plans exist. Either of them entitles you to place two hours per month of long-distance intrastate calls during specified hours for a flat fee. The basic plan, $5.45 per month, lets you place your discount calls between 11:30 PM and 7 AM, Sunday through Friday and between noon Saturday and 5 PM Sunday. The expanded plan, $10.90 per month, extends those discount hours, from 10 PM until 8 AM Sunday through Thursday, and from 5 PM Friday until 7 AM Sunday. Extra time beyond your two-hour allowance is billed in discounted increments of six minutes each: 55 cents each on the basic plan, 27 cents each on the expanded plan. There is also a $4.85 start-up service charge for either service.
- **Michigan** has "Budget-Toll Dialing Service" and "Circle Calling." "Budget Toll Dialing Service" allows you to call anywhere in the state during specified hours (Sunday to Friday, 10 PM to 8 AM, and from 5 PM Friday until 5 PM Sunday) at 30 percent off the applicable toll rates. The cost is $3 a month. "Circle Calling" allows you to call within 30 miles of your home central office from noon to 8 AM for 30 percent off the applicable toll rate. The $3 subscription fee includes an allowance of $1.75 for in-state calls.
- **Idaho's** "Call Thrift" allows you to make either one hour or two hours of intrastate toll calls during the night and weekend hours for either $3.60 or $6.80 a month. There is a 6-cent charge for each additional minute on the one-hour plan and a 5-cent charge on the two-hour plan.
- In **Florida,** the "Value Pack" plan allows an additional discount of 50 percent off the night and weekend rates for intrastate calls. The $4 subscription fee is credited to the first $8 of calls.
- **Massachusetts** offers "Bay State Service," which allows you to make two hours of in-state calls anytime except 9 AM to noon on weekdays for a fee of between $12 and $14 a month (depending on your basic exchange

service area). There is a charge of 5½ cents per minute for all minutes over the two hours.

- **New Hampshire's** "Granite State Service" allows you to make two hours of in-state calls anytime except 9 AM to noon and 6 PM to 9 PM on weekdays for a subscription fee of $10.55 per month. There is a 7-cent-per-minute charge for use beyond the two hours.
- In **Alabama, Louisiana, Mississippi,** and **Tennessee,** South Central Bell provides a service that allows you to place up to one hour of intrastate calls during specified hours for a flat monthly fee, with additional time billed in six-minute increments. In Alabama, where the plan is known as "Measured Home Area Code Calling," a monthly payment of $13.22 lets you call between noon and 6 PM or 9:30 PM and 8 AM, Monday through Friday; or between 9:30 PM Friday and 8 AM Monday. Each additional six minutes is $1.07. In the other three states, the plan is called "Tele-Thrift," and is priced comparably.
- In **South Dakota,** the "Gold Line" service allows you one hour of intrastate toll calls during certain hours for a flat fee of $6 per month, applicable on weekdays between 11 PM and 8 AM, all day Saturday, and between 8 AM and 5 PM on Sunday. For $10 per month, the service is also available on weekdays from 5 PM until 11 PM. For $16 per month, the service is also available between 8 AM and 5 PM, Monday through Friday. Extra time is billed in six-minute increments: 60 cents for the lowest-cost plan, $1 on the middle plan, and $1.60 on the high-cost plan.

Remember: When considering any of these special toll services, make sure that your personal calling habits will ensure that you can take advantage of the discounts. You may want to review a few of your recent phone bills to see whether you'd save anything. Consider the limitations the plans may place on the time of day. And periodically review your calling habits to make sure that any such plan is still saving you money. Ask a phone company service representative to help you perform a detailed comparison of your phone bill under regular toll charges and under the special discount plans.

YOUR LONG-DISTANCE BILL

For many people, long-distance calls make up the largest part of the phone bill. It is easier and quicker to "reach out and touch someone" than to write a letter. Realizing that "the next best thing to being there" can be quite profitable, AT&T spends a lot of money to tell its customers how to save money on long distance. And the suggestions offered by Ma Bell can really be very helpful in saving quite a bit of money—up to a point, that is (but more about that later).

Like other utilities, the phone company must have enough equipment to meet customer demand at its peak level, when the largest number of calls are being made. For Bell this period is Monday through Friday from 8 AM to 5 PM, when the heavy business users are making calls. If the phone company can get consumers to spread their calls out over the entire day, then they won't have as high a peak and they won't have to build as much equipment to help meet the load; this keeps the phone company's costs down and, presumably, consumers' costs down, too. To get callers to call during non-peak times, Ma Bell lowers the price for making a long-distance call during those times when there are fewer calls being made. The lower rates are highly publicized; chances are you've received a copy of the rate card in your monthly phone bill.

The rate chart appearing below demonstrates the long-distance rates and discounts available for interstate (between two states) calls whether you dial them yourself or place your call through the operator (but note there are surcharges placed on calls you don't dial yourself). The first minute of your call is always somewhat higher than additional minutes, although *all* the minutes are discounted proportionally during discount-dialing periods.

Intrastate calls—long-distance calls within the same state—are billed differently since they are regulated by state public utility commissions and not by the Federal Communications Commission. Call your phone company business office for additional information about intrastate rates.

The rate in effect at the moment you place your long-distance call applies only until the next rate period begins. For example, if you make a weekday call at 4:55 PM and talk for ten minutes, you will be billed for

Rate discount periods

Monday	Tuesday	Wednesday	Thursday	Friday	Saturday	Sunday
Weekdays **Full Rate** Mon.–Fri. 8 AM to 5 PM						
Evenings **40% discount** Sun.–Fri. 5 PM to 11 PM						35%
Nights & Weekends **60% discount** Sat. anytime, Sun. (except 5–11 PM), any night after 11 PM						

five minutes at the full rate and five minutes at the 40-percent discount evening rate. This represents a change from the old practice, where the rate in effect at the moment you placed your call was the rate you would be charged for the entire call. (This is still the way intrastate toll calls are billed.)

Sample rates between your city and distant cities are printed in the section on long-distance calling in the "Customer Guide" portion of your White Pages. If you want specific rates from your city to another city, you may also call "0" (a free call). More detailed charts are available from your phone company's business office.

Before they were telling us to "reach out and touch someone," the phone company was telling us to "dial direct and save." The savings on a direct-dialed call over an operator-assisted call are worth noting. Interstate long-distance calls fall into three groups:

Direct-Dialed Calls. These are calls placed without any operator assistance from a home or office phone. The caller must dial the number, and the call is timed beginning when the phone is answered. These calls are the least expensive of all, and there is a minimum charge of one minute. They are timed in one-minute increments, the first minute being a little more expensive than the rest. Here's an example: let's say you're in town X, and you want to call town Y in another state. The rate for the first minute would be, say, 50 cents, and each additional minute 42 cents. If you spoke to someone in town Y for two minutes and thirty seconds, you would be billed for a total of three minutes: 50 cents for the initial minute and 42 cents each for the second and third minutes; total: $1.34.

All long-distance times are rounded off to whole minutes. Any fraction of a minute is rounded up to the next full minute. For example, if you were on the line for two minutes and two seconds, your call would be rounded up to three minutes and billed accordingly.

When you place a direct-dialed call but cannot get through, you can call the operator ("0") and explain the problem. The operator will then place the call for you, but you will not be billed the surcharge for an operator-assisted call.

Operator-Assisted Station-to-Station Calls. These calls include calls placed by an operator at the customer's request (except as noted above), all station-to-station calls from coin phones, collect calls, calls billed to a third number, credit card (now known as "calling card") calls, and hotel guest calls. The caller begins to pay for the call when the phone is answered. The rates per minute are the same as for direct-dialed calls. The caller is billed for a minimum of one minute, no matter how brief the call. The cost per minute is subject to any applicable discounts for time of day, just as with direct-dialed calls. However, an additional surcharge for operator assistance is added to the dial rate in effect at the time the call is placed. You will be billed a service charge of 75 cents for calls to locations within a 10-mile radius. Calls to places between 11 and 22 miles away will cost an additional $1.10 for operator assistance. A service fee of $1.55 will apply to operator-assisted calls over 22 miles away.

"Calling card" (credit card) calls are considered operator-assisted calls, but are billed at a lower rate. The customer will be billed a service charge of 60 cents if the receiving party is up to ten miles from the caller. An 80-cent service charge will be added to the bill if the caller reaches a party 11 to 22 miles away. When the answering party to a calling card call is farther than 22 miles from the caller, a service charge of $1.05 is added to the dial rate. (These surcharges are 25 to 48 percent lower than regular operator-assisted rates.) The "calling card" is useable anywhere in the U.S. or when calling from Bermuda, the Bahamas, and many Caribbean islands back to the U.S.

Person-to-Person Calls. This is an operator-assisted call in which the caller asks to speak to a specific person, department, or office. The same rate applies if the party you wanted to speak with is out but you agree to speak with someone else. Otherwise, there is no charge for the call if you do not speak to the person you wanted. The call is timed beginning when the person you requested comes on the line. The cost per minute is the same as for direct-dialed calls. When your person-to-person call is connected, you will pay an automatic $3 surcharge regardless of the distance of your call.

Person-to-person calls can cost nearly twice as much as other operator-assisted calls, and several times more than direct-dialed calls. Also note that a person-to-person *collect* call is more expensive than a collect call for just "anyone."

When you place a conference call, there is a separate $3 service charge for each connection, in addition to the rates charged for the conversation portions of each connection.

The New Long-Distance Competitors

We've just reviewed what Bell tells you about saving money on long-distance calls. And most people still think that AT&T is the only game in town for long-distance service.

What Ma Bell won't tell you is that there comes a time in a telephone user's life when it may pay to leave Mom. There are now several companies competing with AT&T in the long-distance market: MCI, Southern Pacific's "Sprint" (which is currently being purchased by General Telephone and Electronics Company), U.S. Transmission System's "Longer Distance" (a subsidiary of ITT), Western Union's "MetroFone," and Satellite Business System's "Skyline." They all boast of opportunities for large savings on the long-distance portion of your monthly bill.

Someone unacquainted with these new competitors, which are called "specialized common carriers" (or SCCs), might ask, "Isn't it a duplication of effort for a lot of different companies to be running long-distance lines all over the country? And how can a company that is just a fraction of the size of AT&T provide a similar service for a lower price?" The answer is that these new competitors have built their base by concentrating on routes where long-distance traffic is heavy, so the cost of carrying each call is relatively low. Also, the competitors' transmission equipment consists almost exclusively of computers and microwave links, which they have built themselves or which they lease from other carriers. Thus, these networks can be less expensive to construct and maintain than the cable-based systems that Bell has used for years. There's also another new class of competitors called "resellers," who lease and resell both AT&T's and other carriers' lines. More about resellers in a moment.

Initially, most of the SCC competitors could reach only a limited number of cities. But as they've grown, the number of cities served by their microwave networks has steadily increased, and today most of the SCCs reach 70 percent or more of all area codes in the United States and continue to increase the number of cities served every month. Satellite Business System's "Skyline" is the first to offer service to the entire U.S. over its own network. The other SCCs are phasing in universal service by using Bell's WATS system. But while users of these services will soon be able to call *to* anywhere in the U.S., they will still be able to call *from* only a limited number of places, usually the major metropolitan areas.

How much you can save using one of these alternative long-distance companies depends on how frequently and where you call and the hour of the day you tend to use your phone. Several of the competitors advertise that if your bill exceeds $25 per month for long-distance calls, you could probably save with their system. But with new limited and less expensive options, such as MCI's "Weekender Service," it may save to subscribe even if your bill is considerably less.

To use any of these SCC services, you currently must have Touch-Tone (push-button) service or an equivalent in your home. (This may change in the future, as a consequence of the AT&T/Department of Justice divestiture announcement, which would require the newly independent local phone companies to grant all carriers "equal access" at equal rates.) There is an additional monthly charge by the phone company for Touch-Tone service (check the "Customer Guide" in your local White Pages, or call your phone company business office for details); however, you don't have to rent or buy a Bell telephone to get Touch-Tone service.

If your local phone lines already are equipped to handle both rotary and Touch-Tone calls, you may be able to avoid the need for Touch-Tone service in this way: using a regular rotary phone, you place a call to the SCC's computer; then, to converse with the computer and place your long-distance call, you can use a touch pad converter or a tone generator, held up to the mouthpiece of your rotary phone.

It's reasonably easy to use the SCC systems. You must first dial a seven-digit local phone number (an "access number"), which connects you to the SCC's computer. When you hear a tone on the other end, you then dial a five- or six-digit number (an "authorization code") that tells the computer you're an authorized user and to bill your account for the call. Immediately after dialing the authorization number, you dial the area code and number you wish to call. The SCC's computer in your area then sends your call out over its own long-distance network to a computer in the area you wish to call; the computer at the other end then hooks your call into the local phone network to reach whomever you've called. Each month you receive a bill from your SCC (separate from your regular phone bill) detailing your calls and billing you for service charges plus your calls.

Right now it may seem like you've got to dial a lot of digits to save some money. But in a couple of parts of the country, an SCC has succeeded in arranging for "single-digit access" with the local phone company. Just as you need only to dial "1" to place a long-distance call on AT&T's lines, in certain places you only need to dial "6" to place a call on MCI, or an "8" to call on Sprint, etc. And in the future, based upon plans now being developed by AT&T pursuant to the court-ordered divestiture, consumers will have the opportunity to select a number of long-distance carriers for easy access. Consumers will be given the option to select a primary company and any number of secondary companies, which may be AT&T long lines, MCI, or any other SCC. The primary long-distance company you select will be the one you use when you make a long-distance call from your home, and no matter which one you choose, you'll simply dial the normal ten digits (or eleven if your system requires you to dial "1" first for long-distance calls). Thus, if you were to select Sprint as your primary carrier, you would dial your long-distance calls just as you do now with AT&T's long lines, but your calls would go out over the facilities of Sprint and Sprint would bill you for your calls just as the telephone company does now.

Under the same plan, you will be able to select one or more secondary long-distance companies, and will be able to call over the facilities of those other companies by dialing a four-digit access code, then the ten (or eleven) digits normally used for long-distance calls. The 14 numbers for secondary carriers are still substantially more convenient than dialing the 23 digits now required to make a call through an SCC.

But even as things stand now, the frequent long-distance caller may stand to benefit significantly in exchange for the minor inconvenience of punching a few more buttons. Here is a comparison of the five SCCs mentioned above, showing what each service costs, what it offers, and how they differ. Following that is a chart adapted from a similar chart appearing in *Consumer Reports*; it provides detailed comparisons of the cost-per-minute of calls placed through the Bell system and those placed through the various SCCs.

SCC COMPARISON CHART

	MCI ("Execunet")	SPC ("Sprint")	ITT ("Longer Distance")	WU ("MetroFone")	SBS ("Skyline")
Is there a start-up charge?	No	No	$30 for business	No	$16
What is the monthly service fee?[1]	Supersaver Service[1]: $5 24-hour service: $10 Weekender Service: $1	Res.: $5 Bus.: $10	Consumer Service: $5 Niteline Service: $5 Business Service: $10	Res.: None Bus. 1: $5 Bus. 2: $10	None
What is the min. bill?[3]	No min.	Res.: none Business: $25	Consumer: None Niteline: $14 Business: None	Res.: $10 Bus. 1: $40 Bus. 2: None	$15
What is the billing increment?[2]	One-min. increments. Begins about 45 sec. from start of call	One-min. increments. Begins about 45 sec. from start of call	Consumer and Business: One-min. increments. Begins about 45 sec. from start of call. Niteline: 30-min. increments aggregated over one month (151 min. is billed as 6 ½-hour units.)	One-min. increments. Begins about 45 sec. from start of call.	6-sec increments. Begins when call is completed
How many digits must I dial to make a call?[3]	22	23	23	23[4]	24
How many metropolitan areas are reached by this service?[5]	240	270	112	22[5]	Entire U.S.

	MCI ("Execunet")	SPC ("Sprint")	ITT ("Longer Distance")	WU ("MetroFone")	SBS ("Skyline")
When can I use this service?[6]	24-hour Service: Unlimited usage Supersaver Service: 4 PM–8 PM Mon.–Fri., all day weekends & five major holidays. Weekender Service: 4 PM Fri.–10 AM Mon.	Bus.: Unlimited usage Res.: No usage 9–11 AM Mon.–Fri.	Consumer & Business: Unlimited usage. Niteline: 5 PM–8 AM Mon.–Fri., all day weekends plus five major holidays	Bus. 1 & 2: Unlimited usage. Res.: 6 PM–8 AM weekdays & anytime on weekends.	24-hr. service
Are wrong numbers credited?[7]	Yes, after billing	Yes, after billing	Yes, after billing	Yes, after billing	Yes, on line
Must I give written notice when I want to cancel?	No, 48 hours to disconnect after verbal or written notice	Yes, 30 days' written notice	Yes, 30 days' written notice	Yes, 30 days' written notice	Yes, 30 days' written notice

1. American Express Company offers MCI service to its card members at a 20-percent discount off the monthly fee. Called "Expressphone," American Express card holders can subscribe for $4 a month for Supersaver Service and $8 a month for 24-Hour Service. "Expressphone" is billed through American Express, not MCI. Rates for individual calls are the same as for regular MCI service.

2. You will be billed for a one-minute call even if no one answers if you allow the phone to ring for 45 seconds or longer. Each carrier offers credit for any one-minute charge on your bill that you identify as an incomplete call.

3. Each service can be used from any Touch-Tone-equipped phone in your calling area. Some phones, called "Universal dial" phones, appear to be Touch-Tone but don't actually generate the electrical tone needed for these services. SCCs can test your phone to see whether it can be used on their network.

4. WU offers an "abbreviated dialing" feature that allows you to abbreviate your most frequently dialed numbers. You need only eight digits, instead of the entire phone number, to be connected to the party you're calling. This is a function of WU's network and can only be used to place calls over that network. It carries an additional fee.

5. With the exception of SBS, which uses satellites, the areas served by the SCCs are limited because they use their own microwave lines (and links leased from other carriers). Nationwide service should be available from all the SCCs by the end of 1983, however. This expanded service involves leasing regular telephone lines to reach cities not on an SCC's microwave network. Calls to these "off-net" cities will be more expensive than those made to network cities, although a slight discount will pertain. The SCCs have named these new expanded services as follows: MCI "Omni Service"; SPC "Universal Termination" (for business customers only); ITT "Universal Delivery" (for business customers only); and Western Union "Metroplus."

6. Just like AT&T, the SCCs want to spread their calling load over the whole day to keep their equipment investment requirement down. This accounts for the series of discounts appearing here, and for the inducement provided in some of the monthly users' fees intended to keep residential users off the line during high business-usage hours.

7. AT&T and SBS will give you credit for wrong numbers before you receive your telephone bill. For AT&T, simply call the operator. SBS requires you to call their service representative. The other SCCs will give credit only after the error appears on your monthly bill.

Range of Costs for Calls of 100 to 3000 Miles
(in cents per min.)

	DAY[1] (8 AM–5 PM)	EVENING[2] (5 PM–11 PM)	NIGHT[3] (11 PM–8 AM & weekends)
AT&T (Direct Dial)	(1st min.) 57–74¢ (addl. min.) 37–49¢	34–44¢ 23–30¢	22–29¢ 15–20¢
ITT "LONGER DISTANCE" Consumer Service Business Service	 35–53¢ 30–49¢	 12–19¢ (5–8 PM) 19–31¢ (8–11 PM) 14–23¢	 9–13¢ 10–17¢
Niteline	No service	Flat rate of $7 per hr. billed in 30–min. increments. (One hr. of service equals 12¢ per min.)	
Universal Off-Net cities[4]	36–48¢	22–26¢	14–19¢
SOUTHERN PACIFIC "SPRINT" LTD. Res. Bus. Universal Termination	36–47¢ 32–43¢ 36–48¢	14–18¢ 14–18¢ 22–26¢	10–13¢ 10–13¢ 14–19¢
MCI EXECUNET Regular Service Omni Service[5]	 33–43¢ 36–48¢	 16–20¢ 22–26¢	 12–16¢ 14–19¢
WESTERN UNION MetroFone Metroplus	 29–42¢ 36–48¢	 (6–11 PM) 14–19¢ (6–11 PM) 22–29¢	 10–14¢ 14–19¢
SBS "SKYLINE" Neighboring state All other states	 25¢ 39¢	 13¢ 18¢	 10¢ 14¢

1. SPRINT day hours are 8 AM–9 AM and 11 AM–5 PM for residential service.
2. ITT divides its evening hours for its business service into two sections: 5–8 PM and 8–11 PM. Western Union evening hours are 6 PM–11 PM.
3. ITT weekend hours begin at 11 PM Friday and continues through 8 AM on Monday. All others begin at 11 PM Friday and continue through 5 PM on Sunday, with evening rates applying between 5 PM and 11 PM Sunday.
4. Estimates based on percentage discounts claimed by ITT. These rates apply only to cities not served by the ITT microwave network and that are reached through leased AT&T lines.
5. Omni Service rates are as given by MCI, and apply to calls to cities not served by the MCI microwave network and that are reached through leased AT&T lines.

How to Choose a Long-Distance Service

Choosing the right long-distance telephone company for your needs is going to take a little time and effort, but you will be rewarded with substantial savings when you make the right choice. If you do choose to subscribe to one of these alternative services, remember that you can still place long-distance calls on AT&T's lines simply by dialing as you now do.

The first step is to analyze your long-distance calling habits, paying special attention to *where* you call most often. Then see which companies reach most of the cities you typically call. Most long-distance companies will reach the entire country by the end of 1983, just as the Bell System (and independent phone companies such as General Telephone or Continental Telephone) does now. SBS's "Skyline" already has nationwide reach over its own facilities. (For more information, check the SCC Comparison Chart.)

The next step is to analyze *when* you make most of your long-distance calls. Not all services are available to residential users at all times during the day (MCI, for example, offers a limited service available only between 4 and 8 PM on weekdays and all day on weekends). But in any case, you almost invariably save most when you call in the evenings, at night, or on weekends. If you can limit most of your calling to nights or weekends, MCI "Weekender" service or ITT's "Niteline" might be the best option for you. Keep in mind that most services offered by SCCs are available to you as a residential user, even those labeled "business" services. Your choice should be based on what will save you the most money, given your personal calling patterns and needs.

Depending on where you call and the time of day you do your calling, the cost of placing a long-distance call on one of the competitive services averages about 25 to 50 percent cheaper, when made on their network facilities, than AT&T. The savings are even greater when compared to the cost of placing operator-assisted or calling-card calls over the Bell System. One warning: although the competitors justifiably tout their lower rates, you can expect that they will increase each time AT&T increases its rates.

The different pricing strategies and services offered by the long-distance competitors make it difficult to generalize about cost-saving strategies. You should always calculate your estimated savings based on your actual calling patterns and habits. Remember, your telephone bill will show you the time of day, the length of the call, and the cost for each long-distance call you have made over the Bell System. You should compare what it would cost you to make identical calls over the same period using the various competitive services. When you make that comparison, here are some of the things you'll probably discover:

- The greatest savings over Bell rates occur in calls of short duration because Bell first-minute rates are so high. The longer you talk, the lower the per-minute rate and the less you save using an SCC.
- For most of the carriers, the greatest savings over Bell rates occur during the evening calling hours. SBS's "Skyline," however, saves you the most during the daytime hours, and Western Union's savings tend to be about the same during both the day and the evening time periods when compared to Bell.
- Despite the fact that SCC rates may be more *favorable* during the evening hours when compared to Bell, they're always *lowest*—in absolute terms—during the night and weekend calling periods.
- In general, the greater the distance of a call made during evening and nighttime hours, the greater the savings. During the day, the opposite tends to be true—savings are higher over shorter distances.
- Some services don't save you anything over Bell during certain calling periods, so be very conscious of when you do your calling. For example, ITT "Consumer Service," according to our calculations, would cost 1 percent *more* per minute than Bell for a 10-minute, daytime, 3,000-mile call.
- Remember to average in your monthly service costs in estimating your savings. And if you are considering a service that requires a minimum amount of calling rather than a service charge, consider whether you are likely to meet the minimum. If not, the extra costs are comparable to a service charge.

If you tend to travel and need to place many of your long-distance calls from places other than your home or office, you should note that MCI, SBS, and Western Union cannot be used outside of the city in which you live without purchasing a special "travel card" with a small additional monthly rate. SPC and ITT can. Since you automatically bill your calls to your SPC, ITT, MCI, or WU account just by dialing from any Touch-Tone equipped phone in any city served by the system, you would have no need to make calling-card (credit card) calls, operator-assisted calls, or calls billed to a third number when you call from a pay phone or someone else's phone. This service also allows you to give your authorization code to your children who may be away at school. The kids can call you or other long-distance numbers directly from wherever they are, and the bill goes to you; most of these companies list the calls in each monthly bill grouped by city of origin, so it will be easy to see which of the people using your authorization code made which calls.

If you have message unit or local measured service, keep this in mind: any calls you make over the systems of the competitive long-distance carriers must begin with a local phone call to the SCC's computer. *This is a local phone call, and you will be charged by your local phone company just as you would for any other call in your local calling area.* Thus, if you have local measured service, and you stay on your long-distance call for 15 minutes, you have to add in the cost of a local 15-minute call to determine whether the competitive long-distance service is really saving you money.

If you make many of your long-distance calls from pay phones, remember that your call to the SCC computer will cost you money. Even if your long-distance call does not go through, whether it's because of a busy signal, interference on the line, or an improperly dialed access code number, you will still lose your coin once you've been connected to the computer. And in New York, local pay phones have metered rates, so you will have to keep feeding the phone as you talk long distance.

When you use one of the long-distance competitors, there is also a chance that you will be charged for simply letting the telephone ring. The computers that control and route traffic for the SCCs (with the exception of SBS) automatically begin billing about 45 seconds after your call reaches them—even if no one has answered your call. A phone will ring six or eight times within 45 seconds, so this should not happen often. If it does, the SCCs all claim that you will be credited for any 1-minute charges you claim were the result of incomplete calls.

Keep in mind that the SCCs do not have the same on-line, operator, or billing assistance that is available from Bell. If you reach a wrong number, it is usually necessary to wait until your bill arrives before you can call a service representative and ask for a credit. The exception is SBS, which does have your calling record in a computer and available to their service representatives at all times. SBS, like Bell, can therefore give you a credit at the time the problem occurs.

So, when dealing with the long-distance competitors, demand a copy of their rates per minute, a list of the cities served by their network, and information on their rules and procedures. Then sit down with a recent bill from Bell and compare prices. Don't let one of the SCC sales representatives tell you which system will save you the most money—you already know what you'll be told.

Here's where to write for more information on the competitive long-distance services:

MCI: Write MCI, MCI Building, 17th and M Streets, NW Washington, D.C. 20036. Call toll-free (800) 521-8620 or in Michigan (800) 482-1740.

SBS: Write SBS, John Marshall Building, 8283 Greensboro Drive, McLean, VA 22102. Nationwide, you may call toll-free (800) 698-6900.

SPC: Write SPC, One Adrian Court, Burlingame, CA 94010, or call (800) 521-4949 or in Michigan (800) 645-6020.

ITT: Write ITT, U.S. Transmission Systems, Inc., P.0. Box 732, Bowling Green Station, New York, NY 10004. Nationwide, you may call toll-free (800) 438-9428 or in New York (212) 797-2511.

WU: Write WU, 1 Lake Street, Upper Saddle River, NJ 07458. Call toll-free (800) 325-6000 for the phone number of your local service office.

In each case, you might also check your local telephone directory for a listing under the company's full name or initials, or call Directory Assistance to see if there is a local listing.

Another word on saving money on your long-distance bill. The changes in the telephone industry and the rapidly growing competition for your long-distance dollar are creating numerous new opportunities to save money. It pays to keep alert for changes and new savings opportunities. For example, AT&T has announced that it will launch a new long-distance service in 1983. Under the new service, you will be able to make long-distance calls from special pay telephones for 50 cents for 30 seconds to anywhere in the U.S. Special green telephones will be installed by AT&T in hotels, airports, convention centers, and similar locations. The service is intended for quick calls, and only cash may be used to make the call. No operator assistance will be available.

Long-Distance Resellers

In a 1981 decision, the FCC authorized middlemen to resell standard long-distance and WATS services. This gave rise to a new industry—"resale services"—that attracted many entrepreneurs and more than a few rip-off artists.

This is how a small resale company (we'll call it "Fred's Phone Co.") contracts with AT&T (or with one or more of the SCCs discussed above) to have a certain number of the major carrier's lines "dedicated" to Fred's:

If Fred's leases WATS lines from AT&T, for example, he can take advantage of the fact that the more the lines are used, the cheaper the price-per-minute becomes. Fred's then resells the lines it has leased to residential and small-business customers, whose own calling habits would not warrant the cost of signing up for their own WATS lines. Fred's is able to sell its phone service at lower rates than its customers would pay for AT&T's regular long-distance service because Fred's signs up enough customers to keep its "dedicated" lines constantly busy. In effect, Fred's is buying AT&T's lines and reselling them.

Fred's might lease lines from several SCCs; when one of Fred's customers makes a call, Fred's computer will route the call over the cheapest route (depending on the time of day, distance of the call, etc.). By routing calls the least expensive way, and keeping his dedicated lines constantly busy, Fred's can sell others' phone services and make a profit.

As of mid-1982, the FCC had licensed some 120 organizations to provide resale and sharing of long-distance services ("sharing" is essentially the same as "reselling," except not for profit). However, only about a third of the companies licensed are actually in operation. Most of those companies are concentrated in Texas, Florida, California, New York, and Tennessee, and have revenues of only $250,000 to $2 million—rather small, by phone industry standards. The vast majority of this business comes from businesses; residential customers are just beginning to catch on to these services, primarily during non-business hours.

Resale works much like the SCCs' services, from the customer's perspective: You must have a Touch-Tone phone; you dial a local access number and punch in your own authorization number, plus the number you're calling.

If you are interested in using a resale service, check Appendix II in the back of this book as well as your local Yellow Pages under "Telephone Services," or keep an eye out for resellers advertising in your area. You might also contact the Association of Long Distance Telephone Companies, a trade association of resellers: 2000 L St. NW, #200, Washington, D.C. 20036; 202-463-0440.

You should be cautious about selecting a reseller. Here are some things to consider:

- **Service region.** Not all resellers offer nationwide service; some offer service only in specific regions. And some resellers allow you to place calls only from your home region. For example, if the reseller is based in Atlanta, you may place your calls only from the Atlanta area; the Atlanta-based subscriber could not use the service from other parts of the country. A few larger companies do offer nationwide service by utilizing toll-free 800 phone numbers to gain access to the system; such services, however, are priced considerably higher than local reselling services.

- **Subscribers.** Some resellers cater only to businesses; a growing number allow residential users, but only during non-business hours.

- **Availability.** Not all services are available 24 hours a day, seven days a week. Make sure you can live with any restrictions imposed as to availability.

- **Billing.** Resellers do their own billing on a monthly basis. They provide an individual breakdown of charges, usually based on the distance of the call (some resellers break the U.S. into "regions" or "zones" for billing purposes) and time of day. Most resellers have a monthly minimum charge. Some companies base their rates on the amount of time a service is used. For example, TELTEC, a Miami-based reseller, offers one hour of calling to any of 25 selected cities during off-peak hours for $9.99 a month, or to any city in the country at any time of day for $12.12 a month.

  It's important also to know the increments in which you will be billed. As mentioned previously, Ma Bell has a minimum billing increment of one minute for long-distance calls. Most resellers, however, have the ability to bill on smaller units, such as half-minutes, or even a tenth of a minute. The smaller the increment, the lower your costs are likely to be.

- **Capacity.** Does your reseller have enough lines to enable you to get to the system when you need it? Many people are anxious to call right away when they are ready, and it can be aggravating to have to wait for access. Not all resellers require you to wait, but some firms' capacity is limited by the number of lines they lease. You may want to ask the reseller for references, then call others who have used the system to find out how often they have to wait (and any other comments they may have about the service).

Resellers can save you money and may provide as much access to the nation's phones as you get from Ma Bell herself, although their costs are likely to be a bit higher than the SCC's. However, since some SCCs don't yet reach the entire country, a reseller's services may provide a sensible alternative, if you make enough long-distance calls every month.

Resellers are appearing too fast for even the Federal Communications Commission to keep an accurate and complete listing. The charts that follow are divided by region and give information on resellers currently operating. (See Appendix II for their addresses.) With a few exceptions, resellers' services make sense only for people living in the area where the company is located.

NORTHEASTERN RESELLERS

	Service available from	Installation costs	Monthly service costs	Billing increments	Average cents-per-min. rates for 10-min. call of 100 mi. and 3,000 mi.		Travel features
Alternative Communications Corporation	Rochester, NY	Res.: $10 (applied to 1st 2 bills) Bus.: $20	$5 $10	1 min.	Residential savings are negligible during day, rates are 30% off Bell during eve. Bus. rates are 35% off Bell intrastate & 30% interstate.		None
Combined Network "Allnet"	Pittsburg, PA Washington, D.C. New York, NY	Res.: $7.50 Bus.: $45	$5 $50 minimum	6 sec.	Day 31¢ 41¢ Eve. 11¢ 14¢ Night 8¢ 10¢		"800"-number access from anywhere in U.S.
Penn Telecom, Inc. "DART"	Pittsburg, PA North Pittsburg, PA Butler, PA Perrysville, PA	$15	Day $6 Night $3 (5 P.M. - 8 A.M. and weekends)	30 sec.	Day 32¢ 44¢ Eve. 19¢ 27¢ Night 14¢ 16¢		None
Tel Systems Management Corporation "Call US"	Syracuse, NY Boston, MA New York, NY* Philadelphia, PA*	Res.:$5 Bus.: $60 (Res. is 5 P.M. - 8 A.M. and weekends)	None $50 minimum	1 min.	Day 34¢ 46¢ Eve. 20¢ 27¢ Night 12¢ 16¢		None

* Scheduled to begin service in 1983

NORTHEASTERN RESELLERS (Continued)

	Service available from	Installation costs	Monthly service costs	Billing increments	Average cents-per-min. rates for 10-min. call of 100 mi. and 3,000 mi.		Travel features
United Network Services, Inc. "Custom City Calling"	Baltimore, MD Boston, MA Hartford, CT Newark, NJ New York, NY Philadelpia, PA Stamford, CT Washington, D.C.	Res.:$10 Bus.: $10	$28 annual fee $20 monthly	6 sec. after 1st min.	Day 30¢ 39¢ Eve. 18¢ 23¢ Night 12¢ 16¢		Can call from any network city
U.S. Telephone "Resnet"	New York, NY	$10 annual fee	$10 monthly minimum	1 min.	50% off Bell night & weekends 33% off Bell eve. 25% off Bell weekdays, 6-9 A.M., 11:30-1 P.M., 4:30-5 P.M. 5% off Bell weekdays, 9-11:30 A.M., 1-4:30 P.M.		None

SOUTHEASTERN RESELLERS

	Service available from	Installation costs	Monthly service costs	Billing increments	Average cents-per-min. rates for 10-min. call of 100 mi. and 3,000 mi.		Travel features
Amtel	Memphis, TN Knoxville, TN	Res.: $25 Bus.: up to $75 based on useage	None	6 sec.	Day Eve. Night	35¢ 39¢ 23¢ 26¢ 14¢ 16¢	"800"-number access from outside state
Combined Network "Allnet"	Atlanta, GA	Res.: $7.50 Bus.: $45	$5 $50	6 sec.	Day Eve. Night	31¢ 41¢ 11¢ 14¢ 8¢ 10¢	"800"-number access from outside state
Data Utilities, Inc. "Call US"	Knoxville, TN Oakridge, TN Maryville, TN Lexington, KY	Res.: $25 Bus.: $100 or a $10 monthly fee (Res. is 5 P.M. - 8 A.M. & weekends only)	None $10 monthly or $100 installation fee	1 min.	Day Eve. Night	29¢ 39¢ 18¢ 24¢ 12¢ 16¢	"800"-number access scheduled for '83
Heins Systems "Call Saver"	Raleigh, NC Durham, NC Chapel Hill, NC Research Triangle, NC	Res.: $15 Bus.: $25	$6 ($50 & over) $3 (under $50)	30 sec.	Day Eve. Night	32¢ 41¢ 19¢ 25¢ 13¢ 17¢	None
Microtel "Sunnet"	Miami, FL Ft. Lauderdale, FL Broward, FL Tampa, FL* Dade, FL	Res.: $25 (5 P.M. - 8 A.M. & weekends) Bus.: $75 (24-hr.)	None	1 min.	Day Eve. Night	31¢ 41¢ 11¢ 14¢ 8¢ 10¢	"800"-number access from outside state

SOUTHEASTERN RESELLERS (Continued)

	Service available from	Installation costs	Monthly service costs	Billing increments	Average cents-per-min. rates for 10-min. call of 100 mi. and 3,000 mi.		Travel features
Interstate Communications, Inc.	Atlanta, GA LaGrange, GA Columbus, GA Phoenix City, AL Birmingham, AL Chattanooga, TN	None	Res.: $6 (5 P.M. - 8 A.M. & weekends)	1 min.	Day 31¢ 41¢ Eve. 11¢ 14¢ Night 8¢ 10¢		"800"-number access from outside state or access from any originating city
Network I, Inc. "Network I"	Miami, FL Ft. Lauderdale, FL Boca Raton, FL Broward, FL Gainesville, FL* Jacksonville, FL* St. Petersburg, FL* Dade, FL	$75 for 24-hr. service $25 for eve. (8 A.M. - 5 P.M. & weekends only)	$10 $5	1 min.	in 300 3,000 state mi. mi. Day 16¢ 35¢ 42¢ Eve. 11¢ 20¢ 24¢ Night 5¢ 13¢ 14¢		"800"-number access from outside state
Pacific Atlantic Telephone Hookup "PATH Finders"	Atlanta, GA	Res.: $15 (5 P.M. - 8 A.M. and weekends) Bus.: $75 (24-hour service)	$3 $6.50	30 sec.	Day 30¢ 40¢ Eve. 18¢ 24¢ Night 11¢ 16¢		"800"-number access from outside state

* Scheduled to begin service in 1983.

Company	Cities	Monthly charge	Savings / Options	Billing increment	Rates	Subscriber access from any originating city
Savings Communications Co. "Teltec"	Miami, FL; Dade, FL; Broward, FL; Palm Beach, FL; Boca Raton, FL; W. Palm Beach, FL	Res.: $25 (limited-area calling); Res.: $35 (nationwide calling); Bus.: $85 (large user); Bus.: $40 (small user)	$9.99 (for 1-hr. calling); 12.12 (for 1-hr. calling); 2-,4-,8-, & 15-hr. options; None	1 min.	17¢ per min. for 1st hr. 10¢ per call over 1 hr. + 16¢ (day), 12¢ (eve., night), 14¢ (weekend) per min. / 20¢ per min. for 1st hr. 10¢ per call over 1 hr. + 21¢ (day), 13¢ (eve., night), 16¢ (weekend) per min. / Call Teltec Business office for rate schedules of options / 39¢ during day, 22¢ eve. and night, 17¢ on weekends	Subscriber access from any originating city
Southland Systems	Montgomery, AL; Mobile, AL; Atmore, Al; Ft. Walton Beach, FL; Pensacola, FL	Res.: $10; Bus.: $15	$6 ($50 & over); $3 (less than $50)	30 sec.	Day 32¢ 41¢; Eve. 19¢ 25¢; Night 13¢ 17¢	"800"-number access from outside AL
United Network Services, Inc. "Custom City Calling"	Atlanta, GA; Baton Rouge, LA; Miami, FL; New Orleans, LA; Shreveport, LA	Res.: $10; Bus.: $50	$25 annual fee; $20 (monthly)	6 sec. after 1st min.	Day 30¢ 39¢; Eve. 18¢ 23¢; Night 12¢ 16¢	Subscriber can call from any originating city

MIDWESTERN RESELLERS

	Service available from	Installation costs	Monthly service costs	Billing increments	Average cents-per-min. rates for 10-min. call of 100 mi. and 3,000 mi.		Travel features
Advanced marketing services "Dial America"	Dayton, OH Cincinnati, OH* Columbus, OH*	Res.: $25 (Eve. & weekends) Bus.: Fee based on prior calling record	None	1 min.	Day Eve. Night	32¢ 36¢ 22¢ 25¢ 17¢ 17¢	"800"-number access from anywhere outside Ohio
Combined Network "Allnet"	Minneapolis, MN Chicago, IL Cleveland, OH Cincinnati, OH Indianapolis, IN Detroit, MI St. Louis, MO Milwaukee, WI	Res.: $7.50 Bus.: $45	Res.: $5 Bus.: $50 minimum	6 sec.	Day Eve. Night	31¢ 41¢ 11¢ 14¢ 8¢ 10¢	"800"-number access from anywhere in U.S.
Electronics Office Centers of America "On-Site"	Merchandise Mart & Apparel Center Complex in Chicago	$50	$50 monthly minimum	30 sec.	Day	32¢ 34¢	None

*Scheduled to begin service in 1983. All information is provided by the reseller.

Company	Cities	Installation	Minimum/Charge	Billing increment	Rates		"800" access
LDX, Inc.	St. Louis, MO; Denver, CO; Kansas City, MO	Res.: $10; Bus.: None	Res.: $20 minimum or $4 charge; Bus.: $50 minimum or $10 charge	1st min., then 6 sec.	Day 33¢ 43¢; Eve. 20¢ 26¢; Night 13¢ 17¢		"800"-number access from anywhere in U.S.
Lexitel Communications "MAX"	Cincinnati, OH; Akron, OH; Cleveland, OH; Toledo, OH; Columbus, OH; Dayton, OH; Detroit, MI	Res.: $15; Bus.: (24-hr.) $30 (Res. is 5 P.M. - 8 A.M. & weekends)	Res.: $5; Bus.: $50 minimum + $5 charge	1 min.	Day 30¢ 40¢; Eve. 13¢ 18¢; Night 12¢ 16¢		Subscriber can call from any originating city
Satelco	Chicago, IL; Kansas City, MO; St. Louis, MO	$10	$5	30 sec.	Day 31¢ 38¢; Eve. 17¢ 22¢; Night 11¢ 15¢ (savings vary city to city)		"800"-number access from anywhere in U.S.; direct access in any originating city
Telecommunications Services Corp. "TelSave"	Milwaukee and Brookfield area	$100 (or $5 a mo.)	$5 (or a one-time $100 fee)	6 sec.	Day 30¢ 40¢; Eve. 19¢ 26¢; Night 12¢ 16¢		"800"-number access from anywhere in U.S.
United Network Service, Inc. "Custom City Calling"	Chicago, IL; St. Louis, MO	Res.: $10; Bus.: $50 (both + 2 hrs. service in advance)	$25 annual fee $20 or minimum	6 sec. after 1st min.	Day 30¢ 34¢; Eve. 18¢ 23¢; Night 12¢ 16¢		Subscriber can call from any originating city

SOUTHWESTERN RESELLERS

	Service available from	Installation costs	Monthly service costs	Billing increments	Average cents-per-min. rates for 10-min. call of 100 mi. and 3,000 mi.	Travel features
Business Telephone Systems, Inc. "Value-Line"	20 Texas cities including: El Paso, Amarillo, Longview, Marshall, Austin, Emporia	$35	$25 monthly minimum	1 min.	Monthly bill: $0-500: 20% off Bell rate; $500-2500: 25% off Bell rate; $2500 and over: 30% off Bell rate	"800"-number access from anywhere in U.S.
Long Distance Service, Inc. "LDS"	34 Texas cities including: Austin, Dallas, Houston, El Paso, Brownsville, & San Antonio	Res.: $10 (4 P.M. - 9 A.M., 11:30 A.M. - 1 P.M.) Bus.: $50 (24-hr. service)	None $5	1 min.	40% off all SW Bell intrastate rates between on-net cities; 25% off all other rates	"800"-number access from anywhere in U.S.
Mercury Long Distance	Lake Charles, LA Lafayette, LA Beaumont, TX	Res.: $10 Bus.: $25	$4 $8	30 sec.	Day 37¢ 42¢; Eve. 22¢ 25¢; Night 15¢ 17¢	Subscriber can call from any service city
Satelco	50 Texas cities & 7 major metro areas	$10	$5	30 sec.	Day 31¢ 38¢; Eve. 17¢ 22¢; Night 11¢ 15¢; Savings vary city to city	"800"-number access from originating cities

	Cities served	Sign-up fee	Minimum	Billing increment	Rates	"800" access
TODCO	Austin, TX Dallas, TX San Antonio, TX Houston, TX Ft. Worth, TX Georgetown, TX Waco, TX	None	$5	6 sec.	Day 21¢ 35¢ Eve. 9¢ 18¢ Night 7¢ 12¢	"800"-number access from outside state
U.S. Telephone "Resnet"	46 cities throughout Texas and major U.S. metro areas	$10 annual fee	$10 minimum	1 min.	50% off Bell night/weekend 33% off Bell evening rates 25% off Bell weekday 6-9 A.M., 11:30 - 1 P.M., 4:30 - 5 P.M., 5% off Bell weekday 9-11 A.M., 1-4:30 P.M.	None, but scheduled
United Network Service, Inc. "Custom City Calling"	45 cities including all major U.S. metro areas	Res.: $20 plus 2 mo. in advance ($10) 5 P.M. - 8 A.M., weekends Bus.: $50 plus 2 mo. in advance	$5 $20	6 sec. after 1 min.	Day 30¢ 39¢ Eve. 18¢ 23¢ Night 12¢ 16¢	Can call from any originating city
Westel	Austin, TX Temple, TX	$10	$5	1 min.	Intrastate* Interstate* Day 23¢ 30-35¢ Eve. 17¢ 20-22¢ Night 13¢ 11-13¢ *on-net cities/off-net are 10% off Bell rates	"800"-number access from outside state

WESTERN RESELLERS

	Service available from	Installation costs	Monthly service costs	Billing increments	Average cents-per-min. rates for 10-min. call of 100 mi. and 3,000 mi.	Travel features
Altcom	Seattle, WA Tacoma, WA* Everett, WA* Spokane, WA*	Res.: $25 Bus. (small): $25 (large): $100 (large is 7 hrs. & over calling per mo.)	Res.: $5 Bus. (small): $5 (large): none	6 sec.	Day 38¢ 47¢ Eve. 29¢ 35¢ Night 17¢ 26¢ (10% volume discount)	"800"-number access from outside state
Combined Network "Allnet"	Denver, CO Phoenix, AZ Los Angeles, CA* San Diego, CA*	Res.: $7.50 Bus.: $45	$5 $50 minimum	6 sec.	Day 31¢ 41¢ Eve. 11¢ 14¢ Night 8¢ 10¢	"800"-number access
ISL Toll Systems "Savenet"	Portland, OR	$20	$3 (for 5 P.M. - 8 A.M. & weekends) $5 (for 24-hr. calling)	6 sec.	Day 31¢ 43¢ Eve. 19¢ 26¢ Night 12¢ 18¢	"800"-number access from outside Oregon
Satelco	Los Angeles, CA San Diego, CA San Francisco, CA Phoenix, AZ	$10	$5	6 sec.	Day 21¢ 35¢ Eve. 9¢ 18¢ Night 7¢ 12¢	"800"-number access from outside state

* Scheduled to begin service in 1983

Company	Cities Served	Fee		Billing Increment	Rates			Notes
United Network Service, Inc. "Custom City Calling"	Denver, CO Phoenix, AZ Los Angeles, CA San Francisco, CA Anaheim, CA	Res.: $10 Bus.: $50	$25 (annually) $20 (monthly)	6 sec. after 1st min.	Day Eve. Night	30¢ 18¢ 12¢	39¢ 23¢ 16¢	Subscriber can call from any originating city
United Services Administration "USA Network"	Seattle, WA	$100 monthly or less: $25; $100-275: $45 fee; $275-650: $70 fee; $650 or more a mo.: $125 fee	None	6 sec.	Day Eve. Night	34¢ 34¢ 14¢	39¢ 38¢ 15¢	None
Wylon	19 cities including: Billings, MT Denver, CO	Limited service: $25 (5 P.M. - 8 A.M. & weekends) Unlimited: $150	None	1 min.	Day Eve. Night	27¢ 17¢ 11¢	36¢ 22¢ 15¢	Subscriber can call from any originating city

How to Save on International Calls

Changes in AT&T's tariff that went into effect in 1982 have made it possible to save significantly on international calls.

It is now possible to dial direct to dozens of foreign countries from many parts of the United States. AT&T has revised its rates for "dialable" countries so consumers can make calls with a one-minute minimum; calls to "nondialable" countries still require a three-minute minimum billing. And consumers who live in areas that do not yet have international direct dialing can still take advantage of the one-minute rate to dialable countries by simply dialing Operator and giving the country, city, and telephone number desired.

Rates for international direct-dialed calls are broken into three time-of-day "bands." For example, a direct-dialed call from Los Angeles to London costs $2.08 when placed between 7 AM and 1 PM Pacific Time (the standard rate period); $1.56 when placed between 1 PM and 6 PM Pacific Time (the discount rate period, yielding a 25-percent savings); and $1.25 when placed between 6 PM and 7 AM Pacific Time (the economy rate period, with a 40-percent discount). Each additional minute in each rate period costs less than the first minute, and time-of-day discounts also apply to these additional minutes.

These time-of-day discount rates to dialable countries are available seven days a week.

AT&T has also modified its "calling card" (credit card) to add an "international number" for use when calling back to the U.S. from other foreign countries honoring the card. The international operator can tell you if the foreign country honors the "calling card." All calls placed in this manner will be billed in U.S. currency at the U.S. rate.

AT&T provides additional information on international direct dialing through its International Information Service: 800-874-4000.

OTHER WAYS
TO SAVE

Now that you know about all the options that you can choose in this new competitive telecommunications era, don't forget these few basic tips that every smart consumer should follow:

Read your phone bill. It may sound simplistic, but a surprising number of people fail to do this. Always look over your phone bill (or bills, if you subscribe to competitive long-distance or resale services). Make sure that you have actually made all of the calls for which you're being charged. Be certain you're getting all the services you're paying for. Don't overlook any seemingly incidental charges, such as a substantial charge for Directory Assistance calls that you may not have made.

When you see phone numbers on your long-distance bill that you do not recognize, first check with other members of your family or household. If the call is still in question, call the phone company's business office. They'll give you credit for the call, or help secure additional information to determine if the call is yours.

The competitive long-distance carriers have a similar policy. You will receive an itemized bill that you should check carefully, just as you would an AT&T phone bill. Each of the SCCs claims that it will credit you for any wrong number, incomplete call, or call that was not made by you. Most request that you simply circle the items in question, deduct the amounts from your bill, and attach a written explanation.

Remember, you can be held responsible for all calls made from your phone no matter who made the call. Similarly, you can be held responsible by the SCCs and by resellers for all calls made to your account number. The security of your personal calling code is your responsibility. If at any time you suspect that someone knows your code, you should contact your phone company immediately and request that a new number be issued to you.

Calls made with a Bell System "calling card" (or credit card) are handled much the same way as a call made over a competitive carrier. All calls charged on a calling card will appear separately on your monthly telephone bill. If there are calls listed that you did not make, contact the phone company business office immediately. Although you can be held responsible, the phone company will first try to locate the person who made the calls and, if successful, collect the charges from him or her.

An unfamiliar charge on your phone bill also might be the result of a "third party" charge. Third-party billing is what happens when someone away from your home makes a long-distance call and instructs the operator to charge the call to your number. You are *not* responsible for calls billed to your number without your permission. Operators, however, do not check every call, and you may find that someone is using your phone number to make calls from distant phones. Because of such abuses, Bell plans not to allow third-party calling in the future unless someone is available to authorize the charge. People will be urged to use calling cards instead.

Look through the "Customer Guide" in your phone book. The Bell System operating companies provide good consumer information in the introductory pages of their directories. But the information provided in the front of the book is far from complete. For example, you won't learn anything about the existence of competitive long-distance service providers or other equipment vendors, or about much of the other information that appears in this book. And a good bit of what you find will be subtle or not-so-subtle forms of salesmanship, geared to sell you services and deliver good public relations for the phone company.

Here are a few additional tips:

- Learn how to read the phone bill in your service area, including an explanation of how you're billed.
- Save money by using the equipment left over from the previous occupant of your house or apartment.
- Find out how to handle obscene or harassing calls, and what the phone company is willing to do for you.
- Save money by temporarily suspending your phone service if you're going to be away from home for a month or more.
- Find out which taxes apply to your phone service.
- Find out how disabled persons can secure special phone company service, including teletypewriters and amplifiers for the hard of hearing.
- Find out how to obtain telephone directories for your own service area and other service areas. (Note: You may be charged for directories from distant locations.)
- Find out how to place emergency calls with the greatest speed.

Never forget that phone service is a consumer transaction. Even though the law provides you with certain protections of your rights, these rights are worthless unless you assert them. Use the power of the federal and state regulatory offices that are there to help you. Don't accept phone company explanations of "that's the way things are" until you are satisfied that the answers make sense. And let us know about your failures, successes, and triumphs as a phone consumer. Your experiences may help us to help you better defend your rights, as we all work together to "reverse the charges." (Write us at TRAC, P.O. Box 12038, Washington, D.C. 20005.)

A TELEPHONE CONSUMER'S BILL OF RIGHTS

Don't look in the Constitution. And forget about trying to decipher the mumbo-jumbo in the federal or state regulatory codes.

There really is no universally applicable "phone consumer's bill of rights" on the books today. But a number of attempts have been made to draft one. And even though they aren't yet law (though one of them soon may be), they're the kind of good services you should expect from your phone system.

Louis Sirico, a professor of law at Rutgers University, wrote a fine consumer manual on how to bring complaints against the phone company. Published in 1979 as *How to Talk Back to the Telephone Company: Playing the Telephone Game to Win,* Sirico's book grabbed headlines as the first tool of its kind for telephone ratepayers. (Sirico's book is available for $6 from TRAC, Box 12038, Washington, D.C. 20005.)

In the first chapter of *How to Talk Back,* Sirico said, "Telephone customers outraged by high rates, poor service, excessive charges, and arbitrary policies need an addition to the front page of their telephone books—a Telephone Consumer's Bill of Rights. But telephone companies would not print the list of rights we would propose, because these utilities rarely offer them to subscribers."

Sirico was right. More than two years after the release of his book, there is still no "consumer's bill of rights" in your phone book.

Sirico's manifesto called for the following:

I. The right to high-quality service.
II. The right to service priced as low as reasonably possible.
III. The right to be informed of all service options, including budget rates.
IV. The right to prompt installation and maintenance service.
V. The right to be informed of company requests for rate hikes and how to participate in rate-hike proceedings.

VI. The right to purchase telephone equipment without paying unnecessary extra charges.

VII. The right to accurate, readable telephone bills.

VIII. The right to a policy that does not require excessive customer deposits.

IX. The right to a reasonable policy in collecting future and unpaid bills and discontinuing service.

X. The right to privacy.

As you will note from the preceding chapters of this book, at least some of these rights have become a reality. You can now purchase your own phone from a number of competing sources, and there have been some notable improvements in the detail of your phone bill. The phone company also has improved its policy on deposits, at least by clarifying its criteria. But lots of serious problems remain. Legislative and judicial changes make the future of low-priced phone service (particularly local service) doubtful. Certain proposed reductions in regulation of phone services may make it difficult for consumers to assert many of these rights. And the right to privacy for phone consumers remains very tenuous—and grows more worrisome as phone bills and billing systems are redesigned to retain even more information about consumers' calling habits (for example, with local measured service, it may be necessary for the phone company to retain, for some period of time, detailed computerized logs of your *local* phone calls).

The Bell system began drafting its own list of consumer rights back in 1980, intended at least in part as a response to Lou Sirico's fine suggestions. Recently, Bell published its consumer rights package in pamphlet form, as follows:

Dependable, high-quality services at reasonable prices: The Bell System strives to provide quality telecommunication services and products for all consumers at fair and reasonable prices.

Courteous, helpful assistance: Consumers deserve courteous, helpful assistance in all their transactions with Bell System employees.

Full information about all products and services: Consumers have a right to the information necessary to make sound buying decisions. It is our policy to provide consumers with information they need about our product and service options, including the lowest-priced service available and pricing and payment options.

Choice of products and services: We believe consumers should have free and open choices of telecommunications products and services. When dealing with us the consumer should be given the opportunity to select from all available service options and products.

Safe products and services: We strive to provide and maintain safe, nonhazardous telecommunication products and services to our customers and to the communities we serve.

Telecommunications privacy: We fully safeguard every individual's right to privacy as an essential aspect of our service. We carefully strive to protect communications services from unlawful wiretapping or other illegal interception. Customer service records, credit information, and related personal account information are fully protected.

An accurate, easily understood bill and reasonable billing procedure: We believe consumers should receive an accurate, easily understood bill and one that makes clear when payment is due. Consumers are also entitled to reasonable billing procedures and clear explanations about deposits, late payment of bills, collections, suspension, or disconnection of service for non-payment. In cases of bona-fide emergencies, we try to avoid disconnection of service for non-payment.

Fair resolution of complaints: It is our policy that consumers, wherever located, will have access to a readily available process to provide them with fair resolution of their complaints and grievances concerning services, billing, and other practices and procedures. Accordingly, we openly provide consumers with helpful information about where and how to express their concerns and complaints to the company and to regulatory authorities.

The opportunity to be heard: We believe in listening to consumers and taking their advice, counsel, and criticism into careful consideration in our policy and decision making. We also believe consumers should have the opportunity to be heard on issues affecting our business.

Some members of Congress also have recognized that consumers' rights are jeopardized in this rapidly changing telecommunications environment. In a bill introduced by Rep. Timothy Wirth (D-Colorado), and passed by a House subcommittee in early 1982, there is a section on the rights of ratepayers, stating it is federal policy that users of telephone and telecommunications services:

1. Have access to telecommunications facilities of the highest quality which offer universal and diverse service;
2. Enjoy the benefits of competition, and are protected from monopoly power in markets which are not subject to competitive conditions;

3. Avoid the costs imposed upon the national economy by unnecessary governmental regulation;
4. Do not bear any cost associated with the participation of regulated carriers in competitive markets or with the provision of unregulated services or products by such carriers; and
5. Have access to the widest possible variety of diverse information sources.

Now, all that is a bit harder to understand than Lou Sirico's clearly stated Bill of Rights, or even the Bell draft. But what it all means, simply put, is that the dramatic changes in the telecommunications industry now taking place, and likely in the future, must not have traumatic consequences for the average phone consumer. These legislative terms are meant to ensure that consumers have the broadest possible choice of the best possible services at the lowest possible cost—not an all-inclusive principle, but nevertheless an important one to establish in federal statute. Even though the various consumer rights set forth above have not yet been cast in stone, there is no reason why you should not assert these rights on your own behalf. The well-informed consumer can settle most controversies that come up with the phone company without having to acquire legal counsel or go to small claims court.

Lou Sirico quotes a former Bell system employee: when the telephone company refuses to resolve your complaint fairly, "the name of the game is appeal." Sirico recommends:

> Start with the service representative. If no satisfactory answer is forthcoming, ask to speak to his or her supervisor. If you are still receiving a negative answer, take your appeal to the manager. Meanwhile, complain to the Federal Communications Commission or to your state public utility or public service commission, depending on whether the controversy concerns interstate or intrastate service. Complaints to officers in the company can also help bring positive results. Whether it be a disputed bill, poor service, or an excessive security deposit, resolution of a complaint can be negotiated.
>
> If you find yourself embroiled in a dispute with the telephone company, you should adopt a few obvious procedures of your own. Keep a written record of all contacts with the company and with the [public utility] commission. Be sure to jot down dates, times, names, and a brief summary of the conversation,

as well as any promises made to you. Keep copies of all bills as well as any correspondence you send or receive. If the complaint process begins to drag on, write up a detailed history of the dispute and keep it up-to-date. The written account will keep your record of events accurate, remind others of what they said, and enable you to make an impressive argument. As you move through supervisory levels at the company and deal with the [public utility] commission, be sure to bring your documentation along.

Let's say you've followed Lou Sirico's advice and pursued your complaint through the phone company hierarchy, but with no success. Now where can you turn for help?

If your problem with the phone company concerns long-distance telephone service, the Consumer Assistance and Small Business Division of the Federal Communications Commission in Washington may be able to help you. Contact them at 1919 M Street NW, 2nd Floor, Washington, D.C. 20554; 202-632-7000. The FCC has also created a Consumer Affairs Division within its Common Carrier Bureau to handle telephone problems. Contact: Consumer Affairs Division, Common Carrier Bureau, FCC, 1919 M Street NW, Room 6324, Washington, D.C. 20554; 202-632-7553.

State Regulatory Commissions

The public utility or public service commission in your state regulates in-state telephone services, and can help you with questions or problems when the phone company does not act to your satisfaction. The commissions frequently have consumer representatives who act as liaisons with the local phone company's "appeals branch" to help solve your problem without having to resort to costly and time-consuming proceedings.

Here's a list of the agencies that regulate telephone service in each state:

ALABAMA
Alabama Public Service Commission
P.O. Box 991
Montgomery, AL 36130
205-832-6924

ALASKA
Alaska Public Utilities Commission
1100 MacKay Building
338 Denali Street
Anchorage, AK 99501
907-276-6222

ARIZONA
Arizona Corporation Commission
1200 West Washington, Room 102
Phoenix, AZ 85007
602-255-4146

ARKANSAS
Arkansas Public Service Commission
P.O. Box C 400
Little Rock, AR 72203
501-371-1718

CALIFORNIA
Public Utilities Commission
State of California
State Building
San Francisco, CA 94102
415-557-0647

COLORADO
Public Utilities Commission
of the State of Colorado
500 State Services Bldg.
1525 Sherman Street
Denver, CO 80203
303-839-3181

CONNECTICUT
Dept. of Public Utilities Control
1 Central Park Plaza
New Britain, CT 06051
203-827-1553

DELAWARE
Delaware Public Service Commission
1560 South Dupont Highway
Dover, DE 19901
302-736-4247 or
800-282-8574 (toll free)

DISTRICT OF COLUMBIA
Public Service Commission of the
District of Columbia
451 Indiana Avenue NW
Washington, D.C. 20001
202-659-6000

FLORIDA
Florida Public Service Commission
101 East Gaines Street
Tallahassee, FL 32301
904-488-7238

GEORGIA
Georgia Public Service Commission
15 Peachtree Street, Suite 933
Atlanta, GA 30303
404-656-3982

HAWAII
Public Utilities Commission
of the State of Hawaii
1164 Bishop Street, Suite 911
Honolulu, HI 96813
808-548-3990

IDAHO
Idaho Public Utilities Commission
472 W. Washington Street
Boise, ID 83720
208-334-3143

ILLINOIS
Illinois Commerce Commission
Department of Consumer Affairs
527 East Capitol Avenue
Springfield, IL 62706
217-782-5776

IOWA
Iowa State Commerce Commission
Office of Consumer Counsel
Lucas Building
Des Moines, IA 50319
515-281-5984

KANSAS
Kansas State Corporation Commission
State Office Building
Topeka, KS 66612
913-296-3325

KENTUCKY
Kentucky Public Service Commission
730 Schenkel Lane
P.O. Box 615
Frankfort, KY 40602
502-564-3940

LOUISIANA
State of Louisiana Public Service Commission
One·American Place, Suite 1630
Baton Rouge, LA 70825
504-342-4404

MAINE
Maine Public Utilities Commission
Director of Consumer Assistance
242 State Street
Augusta, ME 04333
207-289-3831

MARYLAND
Maryland Public Service Commission
People's Counsel
301 West Preston Street
State Office Building
Baltimore, MD 21201
301-659-6000

MASSACHUSETTS
Massachusetts Dept. of Public Utilities
Director of Consumer Complaints
100 Cambridge Street
Boston, MA 02202
617-727-3531

MICHIGAN
Michigan Public Service Commission
Director, Consumer Services
6545 Mercantile Way
P.O. Box 30221
Lansing, MI 48909
517-373-3224

MINNESOTA
Minnesota Public Service Commission
Consumer Service Inquiries
7th Floor, American Center Building
Kellog and Robert Streets
Saint Paul, MN 55101
612-296-7126

MISSISSIPPI
Mississippi Public Service Commission
19th Floor, Walter Sillers State
Office Bldg.
P.O. Box 1174
Jackson, MS 39205
601-354-7111

MISSOURI
Missouri Public Service Commission
Director, Consumer Services Division
Jefferson Building
Jefferson City, MO 65101
314-751-3234

MONTANA
Public Service Commission of the
State of Montana
1227 11th Avenue
Helena, MT 59601
406-449-3008

NEBRASKA
Nebraska Public Service Commission
301 Centennial Mall South
Lincoln, NE 68509
402-471-3101

NEVADA
Public Service Commission of Nevada
Consumer Division
Kinkead Building
505 East King Street
Carson City, NV 89701
702-885-5556

NEW HAMPSHIRE
New Hampshire Utilities Commission
8 Old Suncook Road
Building No. 1
Concord, NH 03301
603-271-2452

NEW JERSEY
New Jersey Dept. of Energy
Board of Public Utilities
1100 Raymond Blvd.
Newark, NJ 07102
201-648-2026

NEW MEXICO
New Mexico State Corporation Commission
P.O. Drawer 1269
PERA Building
Santa Fe, NM 87501
505-827-2271

NEW YORK
New York Public Service Commission
Empire State Plaza
Albany, NY 12223
518-474-2528

NORTH CAROLINA
North Carolina Utilities Commission
Director, Consumer Service Division
430 North Salisbury
P.O. Box 991
Raleigh, NC 27602
919-733-4271

NORTH DAKOTA
North Dakota Public Service Commission
State Captiol
Bismarck, ND 58505
701-224-2400

OHIO
Public Utilities Commission of Ohio
Chief, Public Interest Center
375 South High Street
Columbus, OH 43215
614-466-3016

OKLAHOMA
Oklahoma Corporation Commission
Jim Thorpe Building
Oklahoma City, OK 73105
405-521-2351

OREGON
Public Utility Commission of Oregon
300 Labor & Industries Building
Salem, OR 97310
503-378-6600

PENNSYLVANIA
Pennsylvania Public Utility Commission
Director, Bureau of Consumer Services
P.O. Box 3265
Harrisburg, PA 17120
717-783-5391*

RHODE ISLAND
Rhode Island Public Utilities Commission
Div. of Public Utilities and Carriers
100 Orange Street
Providence, RI 02903
401-277-2443

SOUTH CAROLINA
South Carolina Public Service Commission
P.O. Drawer 11649
Columbia, SC 29211
803-758-3621

SOUTH DAKOTA
South Dakota Public Utilities Commission
Capitol Building
Pierre, SD 57501
605-773-3201

TENNESSEE
Tennessee Public Service Commission
Cordell Hull Building
Nashville, TN 37219
615-741-2094

TEXAS
Public Utility Commission of Texas
7800 Shoal Creek Blvd.
Suite 400 N
Austin, TX 78757
512-458-0100

UTAH
Public Service Commission of Utah
Division of Public Utilities
State Office Bldg., Room 613
Salt Lake City, UT 84114
801-533-5511

VERMONT
Vermont Public Service Board
120 State Street
Montpelier, VT 05602
802-828-2358

VIRGINIA
Virginia State Corporation Commission
P.O. Box 1197
Richmond, VA 23209
804-786-8967

WASHINGTON
Washington Utilities and Transportation
Commission
Mail Stop B02
Olympia, WA 98504
206-753-6423

WEST VIRGINIA
Public Service Commission of West Virginia
Room E-217, Capitol Building
Charleston, WV 25305
304-348-2980

WISCONSIN
Public Service Commission of Wisconsin
P.O. Box 7854
Madison, WI 53707
608-266-1241

WYOMING
Public Service Commission of Wyoming
Capitol Hill Building
320 West 25th Street
Cheyenne, WY 82002
307-777-7427

How the New Telecommunications Industry Will Affect You

The phone business and its regulation are changing fast, much too fast for the average consumer to keep fully abreast of it all and understand its implications. The FCC first ruled that, effective January 1983, AT&T may market new phone equipment and certain specialized communication services only through a "fully separated subsidiary." (In response AT&T created American Bell.) By its vote, the FCC sought to remove some long-standing restrictions on AT&T that prohibited them from competing in many parts of the new telecommunications marketplace, while assuring that AT&T would not use its gigantic monopoly and near-monopoly phone services to put the competiton out of business.

This was a momentous decision, but one that would be overshadowed only a few months later by one of the most dramatic announcements in the history of the telecommunications industry.

On January 8, 1982, AT&T chairman Charles Brown and President Reagan's antitrust chief, William Baxter, jointly announced that AT&T had agreed to break up its corporate empire by divesting itself of its 22 local operating companies. In exchange, the new, sleeker AT&T would be free to enter into new businesses (particularly computer-related services) from which it had been prohibited from entering, due to an agreement with the government made in 1956.

While it may take years to determine the impact of an AT&T breakup on consumers, there is little doubt that the settlement will markedly alter the way consumers acquire phone services and equipment.

Residential and small-business phone consumers have an enormous stake in the resolution of the many issues raised by the settlement. The measure of its value will be how well the goal of increased competition in the telecommunications industry is furthered, and how this new competition (and changes in the old order) will benefit consumers.

The most debated issue in the settlement is its potential impact on local telephone rates. Shortly after the announcement of the settlement, banner headlines in newspapers nationwide asserted that local rates were likely to double or triple in a short period of time. Those predictions were based upon likely losses of revenue by the local operating companies from profitable services they no longer would be permitted to provide; for example, the loss of Yellow Pages revenue, and the loss of revenue from leasing telephone equipment to consumers.

Also affecting the long-term cost of local phone service is the issue of whether the newly independent local operating companies will be left fiscally healthy and well equipped to move into a high-technology future. Many state regulators have urged Congress to act to allow the operating companies to enter into businesses in addition to local phone service, as a means of assuring they will have the flexibility to be involved in high-profit businesses. Others, however, argue that to allow the local operating companies to enter into businesses such as long-distance service would merely be to redo what the courts and Congress have been trying to undo for years.

Congress felt compelled to respond to the settlement announcement, and legislation introduced in late 1981 to restructure AT&T was modified to respond to many of the questions raised by the proposed consent decree.

Many of the questions raised by the divestiture and the legislation were resolved on August 24, 1982, when the United States District Court overseeing the consent decree approved the restructuring of AT&T, with some very important modifications. At almost the same time Congress abandoned its efforts to restructure the industry rather than continue to resist an intense lobbying campaign mounted by AT&T against the congressional legislation.

Under the modified final judgment (MFJ), the current twenty-two Bell operating companies will be broken into seven large regional telephone companies. Although these new companies will be independent from one another, there will be a national planning group to assure that the various regional telephone companies can work together in the event of a national emergency and to aid in national defense telecommunications planning.

The two most important changes in the MFJ were a requirement that the

SEVEN-REGION PLANNING MODEL

This map outlines the new regional boundaries, and compares them to the old Bell operating companies.

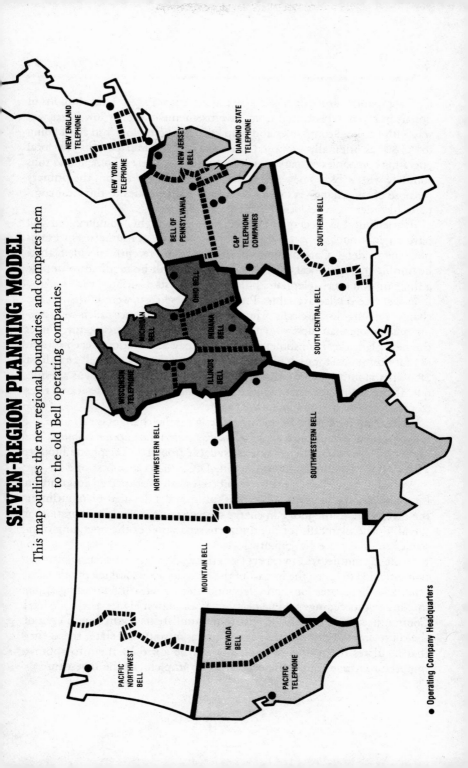

NEW ENGLAND TELEPHONE

NEW YORK TELEPHONE

NEW JERSEY BELL

DIAMOND STATE TELEPHONE

BELL OF PENNSYLVANIA

C&P TELEPHONE COMPANIES

SOUTHERN BELL

OHIO BELL

MICHIGAN BELL

INDIANA BELL

WISCONSIN TELEPHONE

ILLINOIS BELL

SOUTH CENTRAL BELL

NORTHWESTERN BELL

SOUTHWESTERN BELL

MOUNTAIN BELL

PACIFIC NORTHWEST BELL

NEVADA BELL

PACIFIC TELEPHONE

● Operating Company Headquarters

local companies, and not AT&T, keep the Yellow Pages. Thus, billions of dollars in revenue generated from advertisements in the Yellow Pages will stay with the local companies and help keep local rates low instead of going to AT&T as originally proposed. In addition, the MFJ permits the local operating companies to market new consumer premises equipment and thus compete with AT&T's new subsidiary, American Bell. Again, the primary purpose of this change is to provide additional revenues to the local company in order to keep local telephone rates down.

The technical aspects of the restructuring are highly complex and will have an enormous impact on residential telephone consumers. For example, the Federal Communications Commission recently decided that, beginning in 1984, local telephone companies will be required to impose a surcharge on every telephone bill to recover costs associated with making long-distance service available. Previously, these costs were built into the charges for long-distance calls. Thus, frequent long-distance callers were paying much more than those who made long-distance calls infrequently. Under the new plan, every consumer will have to pay $2 additional each month ($4 for businesses) for each phone line. By 1990, the amount will be at least $8.50 per month per line. Although long-distance rates will fall as a result, only frequent long-distance callers will save enough from the decreased rates to make up for the new monthly charge.

A detailed description with charts depicting the changes is contained in a book called *TeleConsumers and the Future: A Consumer's Manual on the AT&T Divestiture*. The book is available from The Telephone Project, TRAC, P.O. Box 12038, Washington, D.C. 20005 at a cost of $4.

Both the judicial and legislative processes can be expected to grind on for many months or years. AT&T has submitted a detailed plan outlining the divestiture to the judge in charge of overseeing the implementation of the MFJ. The plan calls for the complete separation of the operating companies to take place by January 1, 1984.

In the meantime, we can expect Congress again to consider passing legislation intended to lessen the impact of the divestiture on local telephone rates, especially those rates for rural telephone users. You will be reading about important proceedings taking place in Washington, D.C. as the Federal Communications Commission tries to reformulate its regulation in light of the court-ordered divestiture. And at home, in your own state, the agency that regulates the telephone company will be asked by them to approve important changes in statute regulation to implement the divestiture.

It is reasonable, too, to anticipate that, as part of the numerous legislative and regulatory proceedings, AT&T will seek a restructuring or increase in its rates and tariffs. What this can mean for you is much higher telephone rates. Indeed, more than $6.3 *billion* in rate increases were pending or planned throughout the United States *before* the impact of the divestiture began to be felt.

Because residential telephone consumers have such an important stake in the outcome of these various proceedings, it is extremely important that their interests be effectively represented.

How Can Phone Consumers Join Together to Protect Their Interests?

Telephone company spokespeople and executives like to respond to consumer complaints about unnecessary expenditures or about excessive rate increase requests by saying, ''It's just a few pennies more a month.''

A few pennies more each month to you means billions of dollars a year in additional revenues to the telephone company. The average telephone user probably does not object to periodic rate increases—especially those that mean only ''just a few pennies more a month''—if the high quality of local telephone service we have become used to receiving is to continue.

But the changes that are being proposed today are not for just a few more pennies—they call for new charges that will amount to tens of dollars each month and hundreds of additional dollars each year for the average residential telephone user. What's worse, even with these proposed rate increases, there are some serious concerns about whether the quality of local telephone service can be maintained at its current level of excellence.

With all these important issues, and with such large sums of money at stake for the consumer, what can consumers do to have a say in what rates and service will be like in the future?

The telephone companies and other utility monopolies, of course, have the funds, political influence, and expertise to be effectively represented in these state and federal proceedings. Indeed, we are paying the cost of the phone company's lawyers through our telephone rates. But the residential telephone user has little time or money to spend on these complex issues.

It would be silly to suggest that you spend the thousands of dollars needed to hire a lawyer to represent you in any one of these various proceedings, or that you spend the hundreds of hours of study and preparation needed to represent yourself.

Clearly, what is needed to correct the inequity of the current system is a mechanism to allow ratepayers to pool their resources and represent themselves. The idea is really simple, and follows the same pattern used by the phone company itself. The telephone company collects the cost of its lawyers and experts from consumers through a few more pennies each month on your telephone bill. Should not you, the consumer, be allowed to contribute a few more pennies each month, along with other residential telephone users, and have that money go toward paying for consumer advocates, lawyers, and rate experts to represent the consumers' interests in these numerous proceedings?

This idea is the driving force behind legislation which has already been enacted in one state, and proposed in several others as well as in Congress. The legislation is called CUB, for Citizens Utility Board. CUB is a non-profit organization which represents residential and small-business telephone users before state and federal regulatory agencies and legislators. Once created, CUB is permitted—just like the telephone company—to enclose notices in the monthly bill telling consumers about the organization and inviting them to become members by paying a nominal annual membership fee. The annual fees then go to hire experts to represent residential and small-business consumers.

Not everyone has to join CUB. Those who do mail in their membership fee are able to help run the organization by voting for the board of directors or, for the more interested, the opportunity to run for the board.

In Wisconsin, residential utility consumers have been represented by a CUB since 1979. Since its first state-wide mailing, Wisconsin's CUB has grown to over 60,000 members and has helped to save over $14 million for Wisconsin residents. In addition, Wisconsin CUB has conducted studies of several important consumer issues, including the potential economic and social effects of local measured phone service.

Many states are following Wisconsin's lead, and have considered enactment of their own CUB legislation. In California and New York, the state assemblies have repeatedly passed CUB legislation, only to see it die in the state senate. CUB is such a good idea you can expect it to begin to appear as legislative proposals in most states. Efforts have already begun in Arizona, Arkansas, Florida, Missouri, Michigan, New Mexico, Washington, Illinois, and Ohio.

In addition to these states' efforts, however, legislation to create a national CUB on telephone issues was introduced in Congress in February 1982. After Ralph Nader, two former state public service commissioners, and others testified in favor of the national TeleCub at hearings, a modified version was introduced as an amendment to the comprehensive legislation to restructure the telephone industry. Unfortunately, AT&T opposition to the basic legislation resulted in withdrawal of all the telephone-based legislation for 1982 related to the divesture.

Citizens around the country have already begun to join together to work for enactment of CUB laws, including a national TeleCub bill. If you would like to join with them, there are several things you can do:

- Write to U.S. Rep. Timothy Wirth (D-CO), chairman of the House Subcommitttee on Telecommunications, Consumer Protection and Finance; and to Sen. Barry Goldwater (R-AZ), chairman of the Senate Subcommittee on Communications, expressing your support for national CUB legislation.
- Contact consumer groups, labor unions, senior citizen organizations, and the like. Explain CUB to them and ask for their support.
- Write to the editor of your local newspaper, urging the paper to support CUB.

These simple steps require little time and effort, yet can create a powerful consumer organization and save telephone consumers millions of dollars. CUB could make a big difference in your future telephone bills. For more information, or if you want to join with others in this national campaign, contact TRAC, P.O. Box 12038, Washington, D.C. 20005.

APPENDICES

TELEPHONE REFURBISHERS

Telephone refurbishers are companies authorized by the Federal Communiciations Commission to certify telephones in compliance with FCC standards and to issue FCC registration numbers. Most refurbishers will also repair your telephone.

Alabama
Communications Equipment
& Contracting Co.
1500 E. Conecuh St.
Union Springs, AL 36089
205-738-2000

Gray Telephone Repair
Box 40
Lacey's Springs, AL 35754
205-881-6173

Alaska
Alaska Tele-Services
Box 855
Wasilla, AK 99687
907-376-2354

Arizona
V.T.S. Industrial Co.
P.O. Drawer MM
Salome, AZ 85348
602-859-3595

California
Communications Equipment
& Contracting Co. of California
12658 16th St.
Yucaipa, CA 92399
714-795-8911

David Burns
12112 Peoria St.
Sun Valley, CA 91352
213-768-0653

Colin Chambers
1528 Myra Ave.
Los Angeles, CA 90027
213-662-9000

Hegge Services
4554 Caterpillar Rd.
Redding, CA 96003
916-243-8341

Los Angeles Telephone Co.
2335 Westwood Blvd.
Los Angeles, CA 90064
213-470-3344

Telephones Today
7884 La Palma
Buena Park, CA 90620
714-521-4700

American Telephone Repair
Service
906 Center St.
San Carlos, CA 94070
415-593-5677

Phones & Phones & Such
1580 Sebastopol Rd.
Santa Rosa, CA 95401
707-523-3123

U.S. Telecommunications
15346 Bonanza Rd.
Victorville, CA 92392
(619) 245-0281

Thomas-Lynch Industries
15345 Anacapa Rd.
Victorville, CA 92392
714-243-3422

Reintel Industries
444 So. Waterman
San Bernardino, CA 92408
714-885-7521

B & J Enterprises
Box 2355
Costa Mesa, CA 92626
714-631-8800

Pac West Telecom
5757 Pacific Ave. #46
Stockton, CA 95207
209-943-1262

Colorado
Western Antique Telephone
Supply
1535 S. Broadway
Denver, CO 80210
303-778-1717

Florida
Communications Equipment Co.
Box 2580
Leesburg, FL 32748
904-787-7320

Dakel, Inc.
843 Miramar St.
Cape Coral, FL 33904
813-542-3658

Precision Communications Services
2609 DeLeon St.
Tampa, FL 33609
904-728-2730

Telephone Products Co.
Box 6015
Clearwater, FL 33518
813-441-1515

Utility Marketing &
Development Co.
Box 16987
Tampa, FL 33687
813-971-8870

Wintel Service Co.
Box 9200
Longwood, FL 32750
305-834-1188

Zentmeyer Co.
5312 W. Crenshaw
Tampa, FL 33614
813-885-5649

Georgia
Georgia Tel-Electronics
Box 826
Cornelia, GA 30531
404-778-9292

Illinois
Telephone Repair & Supply
1768 W. Lunt Ave.
Chicago, IL 60626
312-764-3817

Communications Equipment
Brokers
321 N. Loomis
Chicago, IL 60607
312-829-8810

Telephone & Data Products
401 Washington Blvd.
Mundelain, IL 60060
312-566-8630

Kentucky
Central Service
Box 186
Kevil, KY 42053
502-462-2146

Louisiana
Telco Communications & Repair
9568 Bonnydune
Shreveport, LA 71106
318-227-8524

Maryland
(Washington, D.C., area)
Stanwood Electronics
9421 Georgia Ave.
Silver Spring, MD 20910
301-588-7788

Massachusetts
Tele-Prime Systems
386 W. Boylston
Worcester, MA 01606
617-852-0480

Minnesota
Gorecki Electronics
620 Industrial Blvd.
Milaca, MN 56353
612-983-3180

Missouri
United Telephone Co.
311 Ellis Blvd.
Jefferson City, MO 65101
314-634-1511

Nebraska
Lincoln Tel. & Tel., Supply Mgr.
330 S. 21st St.
Lincoln, NB 68510
402-477-0716

Nevada
Edwards Industries
Box 11425
Reno, NV 89510
702-786-5353

New York
Bohnsack Equipment Co.
Box 218
Germantown, NY 12526
518-537-6213

Metropolitan Teletronic Corp.
134 W. 18th St.
New York, NY 10011
212-242-6200

Rotelcom
106 Central Ave.
Cortland, NY 13045
607-756-7511

Telephone Extension Corp.
83 E. Central Ave.
Pearl River, NY 10965
914-735-7877

North Carolina
Brown Telephone Repair
3911 S. Boulevard
Charlotte, NC 28209
704-523-3570

Carolina Tel. & Tel., Repair Mgr.
122 E. St. James
Tarboro, NC 27886
919-641-3861

Ohio
Nicho, Inc.
9660 Troy Twp. RD#4
Mansfield, OH 44904
419-884-0123

Phonotronics
15229 So. State
Middlefield, OH 44062
216-632-0236

Refurbco
Box 213
Mansfield, OH 44901
419-526-2200

Comtex
235 Ogden Rd.
Springfield, OH 45501
513-322-6701

Oregon
Phones Plus
656 Charnelton
Eugene, OR 97401
503-687-0111

Pennsylvania
Telephone Engineering Co.
Box 6
Simpson, PA 18407
717-282-5100

United Telephone Repair Center
1430 Trindle Rd.
Carlisle, PA 17013
717-243-6307

Tennessee
Richley Enterprises
106 Leeward Point
Hendersonville, TN 37075
615-824-1014

Texas
Bayless Industries
Box 500
Maud, TX 75567
214-585-2555

House of Telephones
15 East Ave. D
San Angelo, TX 76903
915-655-4174

Netcom
Rte. 2, Box 321
Texarkana, TX 75501
214-794-2471

San/Bar Corp.
2413 S. Shiloh Rd.
Garland, TX 75040
214-840-2710

John Coons
10224 Cardigan
El Paso, TX 79925
915-592-0848

Tele-Service
3205 Richmond Rd.
Texarkana, TX 75503
214-832-3545

Utah
Talk Shop, Inc.
4835 Highland
Salt Lake City, UT 84117
801-272-2562

Virginia
Telephone Systems and Services
Box 1081
Harrisonburg, VA 21801
703-433-2326

Washington
Lippincott Industries
Bldg. S/3 Spokane Industrial Park
Spokane, WA 99216
509-922-1783

West Virginia
Telephone Repair Service
Box 588
Princeton, WV 24740
304-425-2734

Wisconsin
Mid-Plains Telephone Co.
1912 Parmenter St.
Middleton, WI 53562
608-831-1000

Phoneco
Rt. 2, Box 590
Galesville, WI 54630
608-582-4124

LONG-DISTANCE RESELLERS

Allnet Inc.
101 N. Wacker Dr.
Chicago, IL 60606
312-443-1444

Altcom
3055 112th St. NE
Suite 208
Bellview, WA 98004
206-822-6100

Alternative Communications
Corp.
3000 Winston Rd.
South Bldg. E
Rochester, NY 14623
716-442-2904

American Private Lines Service
958 Watertown St.
Newton, MA 02165
617-965-5600

Amtel
207 Summit
Memphis, TN 38104
901-274-3620

Call U.S.
2104 United American Plaza
Knoxville, TN 37929
615-525-2666

Dial America
Suite 910, Talbott Tower
Dayton, OH 45402
513-224-9764

Electronic Office Centers
of America
One Woodfield Place
Suite 415
Schaumburg, IL 60195
312-843-8870

Heins Systems
P.O. Box 981
Sanford, NC 27330
919-774-4145

Interstate Communications
P.O. Box 191
910 First Ave.
West Point, GA 31833
404-645-1013

LDS Inc.
4600 Broadway
San Anotonio, TX 78209
512-828-2269

LDX Inc.
Suite 220
900 Walnut St.
St. Louis, MO 63102
314-621-1199

Lexitel
30300 Telegraph Rd.
Suite 350
Birmingham, MI 48010
313-647-6920

Mercury Inc.
P.O. Box 2215
Sulphur, LA 70663
318-439-3672

Microtel
9040 S.W. 152 St.
Miami, FL 33157
305-233-8333

Network I Inc.
3800 S. Ocean Dr.
Suite 212
Hollywood, FL 33019
305-947-9231

P.A.T.H. Finders
215 Piedmont Ave.
Suite C-5
Atlanta, GA 30308
404-659-6007

Penn Telecom Inc.
GPO Drawer B
Gibsonia, PA 15044
412-443-9500

Satelco
1 Satelco Plaza
100 Taylor
San Antonio, TX 78701
512-226-2226

Savenet
607 Morgan Bldg.
720 SW Washington St.
Portland, OR 97205
503-241-0090

Southland Systems Inc.
201 S. Pensacola Ave.
Atmore, AL 36502
205-666-3830

Telecommunications Services Co.
675 Brookfield Rd.
Brookfield, WI 53005
414-784-6752

Tel Systems Management Corp.
7000 E. Genesee St.
Linden Office Park
Bldg. B
Fayetteville, NY 13066
315-446-7933

Teltec
21000 NE 28th Ave.
Miami, FL 33180
305-932-3031

TODCO
106 E. 6th St.
Austin, TX 78701
512-479-0000

United Network Services
13612 Midway #260
Dallas, TX 75234
214-385-1211

United Services Administration
405 Seattle Tower Bldg.
Seattle, WA 98107
206-223-0521

WesTel
1122 Colorado
Austin, TX 78701
512-474-6266

U.S. Telephone Communications
108 S. Akard St.
Dallas, TX 75202
800-517-4105 Ext. 22

Wylon
235 N. Wolcott
Casper, WY 82502
307-266-3627

Value-Line, Division of Business
Telephone Systems
713 W. St. Johns
Austin, TX 78752
512-459-1100

TELEPHONE COMPANIES

The Telephone Companies

American Telephone &
Telegraph Co.
195 Broadway
New York, NY 10007
212-393-1000

Continental Telephone Corporation
56 Perimeter Center East
Atlanta, GA 30346
404-391-8000

United Telecommunications
PO Box 11315
Kansas City, MO 64112
913-676-3000

GTE International
1 Stamford Forum
Stamford, CT 06904

Bell Operating Companies

American Bell Consumer Products
5 Wood Hollow Rd.
Parsippany, NJ 07054
800-555-8111

AT&T
Long Lines Department
Bedminister, NJ 07921
201-234-4000

New England Telephone
185 Franklin St.
Boston, MA 02107
617-743-7800

Southern New England
Telephone
227 Church St.
New Haven, CT 06506
203-771-5200

New York Telephone
1095 Avenue of the Americas
New York, NY 10036
212-395-2121

New Jersey Bell
540 Broad Street
Newark, NJ 07101
201-649-9900

Bell Telephone of Pennsylvania
One Parkway
Philadelphia, PA 19102
215-466-9900

Chesapeake & Potomac
Telephone
930 H Street NW
Washington, D.C. 20001
301-445-3436

Chesapeake & Potomac Telephone
of Maryland
Constellation Place, 1 East Pratt St.
Baltimore, MD 21202
301-539-9900

Chesapeake & Potomac Telephone
of Virginia
703 East Grace St.
Richmond, VA 23219
804-772-2000

Chesapeake & Potomac Telephone
of West Virginia
1500 MacCorkle Ave. SE
Charleston, WV 25314
304-343-9911

Southern Bell
Hurt Building, PO Box 2211
Atlanta, GA 30301
404-529-8611

South Central Bell
600 North 19th St.
Birmingham, AL 35203
205-321-1000

Ohio Bell
100 Erieview Plaza
Cleveland, OH 44114
216-822-9700

Cincinnati Bell
225 East Fourth St., PO Box 2301
Cincinnati, OH 45201
513-397-9900

Michigan Bell
444 Michigan Avenue
Detroit, MI 48225
313-223-9900

Indiana Bell
240 North Meridian St.
Indianapolis, IN 66204
317-265-2266

Wisconsin Telephone
722 North Broadway
Milwaukee, WI 53202
414-456-3000

Illinois Bell
225 West Randolph St.
Chicago, IL 60606
312-727-9411

Northwestern Bell
100 South 19th St.
Omaha, NE 68102
402-422-2000

Southwestern Bell
1010 Pine St.
St. Louis, MO 63101
314-247-9800

Mountain States Telephone
931 Fourteenth St.
Denver, CO 80202
303-624-2424

Pacific Northwest Bell
1600 Bell Plaza
Seattle, WA 98191
206-345-2211

Pacific Telephone
140 New Montgomery Street
San Francisco, CA 94105
415-542-9000

Western Electric Company
222 Broadway
New York, NY 10038
212-669-2345

Bell Telephone Laboratories
600 Mountain Ave.
Murray Hill, NJ 07974
201-582-3000

WHERE TO GO FOR HELP

Federal

Federal Communications
Commission
Office of Consumer Assistance
1919 M St. NW
Washington, D.C. 20554
202-632-7000

House Communications
Subcommittee
B-331 Rayburn House Office
Building
Washington, D.C. 20515
202-225-9304

Senate Communications
Subcommittee
130 Russell Senate Office
Building
Washington, D.C. 20510
202-224-8144

State

An up-to-date list of state
regulatory agencies appears
in the body of this book.

Consumer Groups

Consumer Federation of America
1314 14th Street NW
Washington, D.C. 20005
202-387-6121

Congress Watch
204 Pennsylvania Ave. SW
Washington, D.C.
202-546-4996

Consumers Union
1511 K St. NW
Washington, D.C. 20005
202-783-6130

American Association of Retired
Persons
1909 K St. NW
Washington, D.C. 20049
202-728-4355

New York Public Interest
Research Group
9 Murray
New York, NY 10007
212-349-6460

Florida Consumers Federation
1101 Stillwater Dr.
Miami Beach, FL 33141
305-861-7539

Toward Utility Rate Normalization
693 Mission Street
San Francisco, CA 94105
415-543-1576

Telecommunications Consumer
Coalition
105 Madison Avenue
New York, NY 10016
212-683-5656

The Telephone Project
TRAC
Box 12038
Washington,, D.C. 20005
202-462-2520